Also by John Sineno
The Firefighter's Cookbook

THE NEW

Firefighter's Cookbook

JOHN SINENO

A FIRESIDE BOOK   Published by Simon & Schuster

New York London Toronto Sydney Tokyo Singapore

FIRESIDE
Rockefeller Center
1230 Avenue of the Americas
New York, NY 10020

FIRESIDE and colophon are registered trademarks
of Simon & Schuster Inc.

Designed by Bonni Leon-Berman

Manufactured in the United States of America

10 9 8 7 6 5 4 3 2

Library of Congress Cataloging-in Publication Data

The new firefighter's cookbook / [edited by] John Sineno.
        p.   cm.
    "A Fireside book."
    Includes index.
    1. Cookery.   I. Sineno, John.
  TX714.N493   1996
  641.5—dc20   95-47547   CIP

ISBN 0-684-81859-0

In memory of my son, Thomas

To my wife, Pauline

To my good friend Jack Meara and all my firefighter family of yesterday and today.

But most of all I don't want to forget the person with the toughest career in the world—the person who chooses to be a housewife and mother—because where would we be without mothers? God bless them all, and thank you, Mom.

Contents

Acknowledgments

Little did I know that thirty-eight years ago when I walked into a city job that my claim to fame would be a cookbook.

In the ten years since the original *Firefighter's Cookbook* was published (Vintage, 1986), firefighters and their families have asked if they can give me their stories and recipes for a follow-up book. *The New Firefighter's Cookbook* is a collection of both—the best of the old and the contributions of the new. Writing this book is a very personal gesture both for me and for all those who have contributed, because it contains the thoughts, ideas, and memories of a firefighting family I hold as close to my heart as my very own family.

Since I'm a retired firefighter with a love of cooking, it's natural I'd feel more comfortable in a firehouse kitchen than perched in front of a typewriter. Therefore I find it necessary to acknowledge, with a deep sense of gratitude, those persons who helped me make this volume (and the first) possible.

Phil Donahue, who granted me national television exposure ten years ago.

My Simon & Schuster editor, Sydny Weinberg Miner, and her lovely assistant, Erin Cartwright, and Susan Fleming Holland for their patience.

Harry Ahearn, my friend and colleague and author of *Ghetto Firefighter.*

My good friend Bob Smith, a volunteer firefighter and fellow director of the New York Firefighters' Burn Center Foundation.

Danny Prince and all the members of Engine 276, Ladder 156, and the 33 Battalion.

Joe DiPinto and Billy Falls for their help and support during the writing of this book, and all the people, from all over the country—and even Italy—who have helped by giving me their recipes and stories.

My daughter Michelle for her patience in trying to interpret my handwriting and that of all the others, and for her diligence in typing the many recipes and stories that went into this book.

My niece, Margaret Bua-Lanza, with special thanks for her help in preparing the book for press.

Finally, my ever-understanding wife, Pauline, and last but certainly not least, Mama Sineno, whose Neapolitan love of cooking inspired most of my menus.

Preface

When I was appointed to the New York City Fire Department in 1962 and assigned to its probationary school, I had no particular concern about firehouse locations, hazardous or otherwise. It was my wife who paced the floor, concerned about the risks associated with certain parts of New York City. She was amazed at my cavalier attitude—and so was I once I found out that I'd been assigned to the "Fire Factory."

The Fire Factory still stands at 114th Street and Fifth Avenue in the heart of Harlem, housing the apparatus of Engine 58 and Ladder 26. At the time of my transfer to that busy engine unit, it was, and remained for many years, the busiest fire company on the face of the earth. And since the units there were so busy—and since practice does make perfect—this particular firehouse has some of the finest professional firefighters ever gathered under one roof. And some of the hungriest.

I retired in 1990, after the publication of the *Firefighter's Cookbook*. A great deal has happened in my life since I wrote that first cookbook, but one thing remains constant, and that is my devotion to my firefighting family and to cooking.

After thousands of runs made and fires fought, countless meals prepared—some good, some ordinary, a few sensational—the Fire Factory is still my home away from home. It is most certainly the place where I performed the role that gave me my greatest satisfaction, serving as a competent professional firefighter while meeting the culinary demands of an always-hungry group of muscular, raucous, and often profane group of characters. And, all these years later, if given a choice

of assignments, the Fire Factory and its ever-ravenous crew would still be my selection.

Walking into a firehouse for the first time is a rather strange experience, or at least it was for me. I was concerned about starting off on the right foot. What would be expected of me? Would I be capable of the job? But the only question Raymond Kelly, then captain of Ladder 26, asked me was, "Can you cook?"

When I answered yes, Captain Kelly, a man of deep religious conviction, believed his prayers begging for deliverance from what passed for food in his platoon had finally been answered. He immediately told me some of the outrages that had been perpetrated on him and his crew in the name of cooking—and I had to agree that outrages they were.

Despite the great joy I get from cooking good meals for my co-firefighters, I feel compelled to say something about the treatment generally given the department chefs. Some people seem to feel that a firehouse cook has to be harassed during the preparation of a meal to ensure a really topnotch result. I beg to differ. Smart-aleck comments comparing the odors wafting from the kitchen with those coming from a stable are not appreciated, nor is it necessary to refer to meatloaf as Ken-L Ration. Further, constant harassment concerning the length of time spent preparing the meal is as unwelcome as the continued criticism regarding the rising costs of ingredients. (Since each firefighter must pay for his or her own meals, cost *is* always a factor. However.) And as for those never-ending complaints from the non-Italian elements assigned to the firehouse concerning the use of garlic . . . well, you can check with my grandmother if you don't think garlic is good for you.

My grandmother is an ancient lady of immense proportions who deserves credit for a large number of the recipes included in this book. Since I'm a modest five feet eight inches, there are many times when I'd really love to be built like her. It would be nice to look some six-foot-five behemoth in the eye and say, "Sit down, shut up, and eat!" Or, as Grandma would say, *"Mangia, mangia!"*

That's what I say to you. *Mangia.* Eat and enjoy. And if it doesn't come out right the first time around, get a friend to harass you on your second try; who knows, perhaps the guys in the firehouse are right. Riding the chef might just be that extra ingredient needed for a superlative meal. It's worth a shot—after all, nothing ventured, nothing gained. Eat hearty!

A Special Association
The New York Firefighters' Burn Center Foundation

Recognizing the trauma associated with massive burns, the New York Firefighters' Burn Center Foundation, an organization of professional and volunteer firefighters, have banded together to help make possible adequate medical care for the most neglected of the hospitalized—the victim of massive burns.

Aware that persons receiving third-degree burns in excess of 25 percent of their anatomy are for all practical purposes dead unless transported to a burn center—*not just any hospital but vitally and necessarily a burn center*—these men and women, whose lives are so closely entwined with such victims, have devoted their time, their energy, and no inconsiderable amount of their own funds toward the establishment and maintenance of the burn center at the New York Hospital–Cornell Medical Center at Sixty-eighth Street and York Avenue in New York City.

This ultramodern unit—open to all, regardless of race, creed, or economic circumstance—is under the direction of, and staffed by, a team of eminent, full-time, nationally recognized burn treatment experts.

For information, contact The New York Firefighters' Burn Center Foundation, c/o Ladder 61.21 Asch Loop, Bronx, NY 10475.

From John Sineno

One day while on duty I received a call on the department telephone from a man who introduced himself as Robert Hine, president of the Harvard Business Club. He said he had received permission from the Fire Commissioner to have some of his club members visit Engine 58. He also said he'd heard that I was a pretty good cook and asked if I might prepare a meal for his group when they came to visit. "Sure," I said, "why not?"

Actually, I thought the call was from one of those firehouse jokesters who constantly plague the unwary with their practical jokes. The supposed Mr. Hine then said he'd visit with his group the following Thursday. "Good, I'll see you then," I said, thinking all the while that I'd handled this particular gagster quite well.

Then it suddenly dawned on me. What if this guy was for real? To be on the safe side, I went upstairs to the officers' room and asked if they'd heard about a visit supposedly set up by the Commissioner's office. Both lieutenants said they'd heard nothing about a visit from a Mr. Hine or anyone else. So, I thought, it's all a gag.

The following Thursday, at about 5:45 P.M., Engine 58 returned to quarters from a run. As the rig headed up the street, I noticed a distinguished-looking man standing in front of the firehouse. As I mounted the pumper, the man walked up to me, extended his hand, and said, "Hi, I'm Robert Hine; my group will be here shortly."

His group turned out to consist of eighty men and women, and if you think firefighters are fast when they respond to an alarm, you should have seen us doing the shopping, preparation, and cooking we did to feed our illustrious visitors on time.

It all turned out quite well, everyone really enjoying the meal and the evening. As he was leaving, Mr. Hine asked if there was anything he could do for the firefighters to show his appreciation. I told him two other firefighters, Jack Meara and Joe Hickey, and I were trying to establish a burn center in New York City. We felt that too many fire victims were succumbing to their injuries and that a really first-class burn center could significantly reduce fatalities. Mr. Hine asked me to arrange a meeting of all concerned so he could be of assistance in the project.

A week later, steadfast in his promise of help, Robert Hine and his brother Ed, a corporation lawyer, joined firefighters Joe

Hickey, Jack Meara, and myself at the quarters of Engine Company 58, in the first of a series of meetings that resulted in the formation and incorporation of the New York Firefighters' Burn Center Foundation.

At this time New York Hospital–Cornell Medical Center was in the process of trying to establish a burn center and asked the New York Firefighters' Burn Center Foundation to support its efforts. A meeting was arranged in the Co-Op City Firehouse, Ladder Company 61, with Drs. David Thompson and Thomas Shires attending as representatives of New York Hospital. An agreement was reached—of course over a few bowls of rice pudding and some cheesecake—that a joint effort would be made to convince the Health and Hospitals Corporation of the dire need for a burn center in the metropolitan area.

To this end the firefighters presented 11,000 signatures to the Health and Hospitals Corporation; New York Hospital promised millions of dollars and its expertise.

As a result, one of the foremost burn centers in the world was successfully established in New York Hospital. Firefighters refer to it as "the Miracle on 68th Street."

From G. Tom Shires, M.D.

In 1976 New York State did not have a burn center. A major burn center had never been developed in a private, nonprofit hospital, primarily because of the cost. The development of a burn center is multifaceted, requiring medical and widespread community support.

Because of the obvious need for such a facility, Dr. David Thompson, director of New York Hospital, agreed to supply financial and medical support for start-up of a major burn center. This included building and equipping a dedicated center with M.D., R.N., Physical Therapy, Occupational Therapy, and other support services such as Nutrition.

The New York Firefighters' Burn Center Foundation had been working hard to develop a center in New York State without success. At the invitation of the president of the New York Firefighters' Burn Center Foundation, Joe Hickey, I met with him and several foundation members at Engine 66, Ladder 61 Firehouse at Co-Op City. We enjoyed a buffet, ending with rice pudding by John Sineno. While I "pigged out" on the pudding, we all came to know and trust each other. The firefighters then supplied the essential community support, and ninety days later the New York Hospital–New York Firefighters' Burn Center Foundation was born.

This center then became the largest burn center in the world, with over 1,000 admissions and 10,000 outpatient visits annually with excellent results.

Without the rice pudding and community support from the New York Firefighters' Burn Center Foundation, the New York Hospital Burn Center might never have come to pass. We owe a tremendous debt to John (and his rice pudding) for creating an atmosphere of camaraderie and cooperation.

Appetizers
AND Soups

APPETIZERS

Taco Dip/*Yokley*

Vegetable Dip/*Elliott*

Baked Mussels/*Sineno*

Corton/*Dionne*

Baked Clams Bellissimo/*Kent*

Salmon Mousse/*Ginley*

Shrimp Mold/*Rella*

Crab Rollups/*Prince*

Crab-Stuffed Mushrooms/*Ginley*

Zucchini Appetizer/*Reed*

Scungilli (Conch) Salad/*Sineno*

SOUPS

Boro-Wide Chicken Soup/*D'Attore*

Chicken Rice Soup/*Sineno*

Chicken and Escarole Soup/*Sineno*

Low Tide Soup/*Solimeno*

Carmela's Special Bean Soup/*Ciance*

Firehouse Bean Soup/*Smith*

Arizona Mountain Soup/*Schwerdt*

Beef Barley Vegetable Soup/*Kessler and Kessler*

Goulash Soup/*White*

Tortellini Meatball Soup/*Buttino*

Turkey Albondigas Soup/*Wood*

Vegetable Soup Express/*d'Emic*

Potato Soup/*Schwerdt*

New York Clam Chowder/*Stack*

Maxie Pearl's Chowder/*Kessler and Kessler*

Manhattan Fish Chowder/*Schwerdt*

TACO DIP

Be careful—guests will dive into this one and won't want much dinner! It's that good!

SERVINGS: PARTY SIZE

1 large can refried beans
1 jar salsa (medium hot)
1 can chopped olives, drained
1 can (4 ounces) diced peeled green chilies, drained
2 avocados, peeled, pitted, and mashed
1 container (16 ounces) sour cream
3 hot carrot slices
3 onion rings
1 jalapeño pepper
Grated cheddar cheese
Tortilla chips

Mix the refried beans with ¼ cup of the salsa. Spread the mixture over the bottom of a serving bowl. Layer with chopped olives, then diced green chilies, salsa, mashed avocados, and sour cream. Garnish the center of the dip with the hot carrots, each within an onion ring, and the jalapeño on top. Sprinkle grated cheddar cheese around the perimeter.

Serve with tortilla chips.

Capt. Richard Yokley
Engine 12, Bonita, California

VEGETABLE DIP

SERVINGS: 12–16

½ cup chili sauce
½ cup vegetable oil
⅓ cup vinegar
1 teaspoon Worcestershire sauce
1 medium onion, finely chopped
1 teaspoon salt
¼ to ½ cup sugar

Mix all the ingredients in a blender until smooth. Chill. Serve with any vegetable or over a salad.

Sgt. Richard Elliott
Volunteer Fire Department, Clarksville, Virginia

BAKED MUSSELS

SERVINGS: YOUR CHOICE

Fresh mussels, cleaned and debearded, in amount desired
¼ to ½ cup water
Seasoned bread crumbs
Melted margarine
Marinara sauce

Preheat the oven to 375° F.

Put the mussels in a frying pan with the water and steam open, covered. Once the mussels are opened, drain off the liquid. Remove one part of the shell and discard. Place the mussels, in shells, in a baking pan and top with bread crumbs. Drizzle with margarine. Pour marinara sauce over the mussels and place in the oven for 10 to 15 minutes.

Serve immediately.

John Sineno, retired
Engine 58, F.D.N.Y

This spread is also spelled Gorton or Creton in Nova Scotia and is sometimes made there using ground beef. It's excellent on English muffins, fresh bread, or even crackers. A good in-between-runs, on a busy night, meal or snack!

SERVINGS: 16–20

1 fresh pork shoulder (about 5 pounds) or 4 pounds ground pork
4 cups water
1 large onion, chopped
Salt
1 level tablespoon allspice per cup of pork

If a pork shoulder is used, cook it overnight in a Crock-Pot and grind up, fat and all, in the A.M. This produces excellent flavor, as the bone-in cooking method is best. If using ground pork, put 1 cup of water for each cup of ground pork into an uncovered pot and slow-simmer until almost all the water is evaporated. (Do not try to do *this* in the Crock-Pot!) Add 1 teaspoon of salt at a time to the cooked pork until you get it to your taste. Then add 1 level tablespoon of allspice per cup of pork. Excess fat can be skimmed off, and the spread can be put into containers. Cool and refrigerate.

For a smoother spread, you can beat it with a hand mixer after it is all cooked and before it is put into containers.

Nelson Dionne
Car 21, Salem, Massachusetts

BAKED CLAMS BELLISSIMO

SERVINGS: 12

3 tablespoons vegetable oil
2 tablespoons butter
1 small onion, finely chopped
2 garlic cloves, minced
1 pint shucked clams, minced, liquid reserved
½ cup dry white wine
2 tablespoons minced fresh parsley
1 tablespoon olive oil
¾ teaspoon white pepper
12 cherrystone clam shells, scrubbed clean
1 cup seasoned bread crumbs

Preheat the oven to 375° F.

Heat the vegetable oil and butter in a skillet. Add the onion and garlic and sauté over medium heat until golden. Drain the clam liquid into the onion mixture, stir in the wine, and simmer for about 5 minutes.

Mix in the clams, parsley, olive oil, and pepper. Heat thoroughly. Spoon into the clam shells and top with the bread crumbs. Bake for about 15 minutes.

Cecil Kent
Ladder 156, F.D.N.Y.

SALMON MOUSSE

SERVINGS: 20

2 envelopes unflavored gelatin
½ cup cold water
2 cans (15 ounces each) pink salmon, drained and liquid reserved
1 cup sour cream
1 cup mayonnaise
¼ cup lemon juice
1 teaspoon salt
1 teaspoon paprika
1 teaspoon hot pepper sauce
Lettuce and lemon wedges for garnish

Soften the gelatin in the water, with salmon liquid added to total 1 cup. Stir over medium heat until the gelatin dissolves. Cool. Place in a blender with the remaining ingredients (except the garnish) and blend till smooth. Pour into a lightly oiled 8-cup mold, cover, and chill until set. Turn the mold onto a lettuce-lined plate; top with lemon wedges.

Joe Ginley, retired
Engine 8, F.D.N.Y.

SHRIMP MOLD

Serve the mold with crackers, potato chips, or pretzels.

SERVINGS: 8-10

3 packages (3 ounces each) Philadelphia cream cheese
1 can tomato soup
1½ packages unflavored gelatin
3 cans (4½ ounces each) deveined shrimp, drained
1 cup mayonnaise
1 cup finely chopped celery
1 bunch green onions, stems only, chopped

Keep the cream cheese out to soften. Heat the soup over low heat and add the cream cheese. Simmer till the cheese is melted. Dissolve the gelatin in ¼ cup cold water and add to the tomato soup along with the remaining ingredients. Stir. Pour into a lightly greased mold. Chill overnight.

Danny Rella
Engine 91, F.D.N.Y.

We were on the *Phil Donahue Show* for the second time and were asked to make something different from the last time. We were not sure if the entire show would be devoted to the cookbook like the first time, so I prepared two dishes—homemade manicotti and crab rollups. The manicotti was in the book; the crab rollups, however, were not.

Prior to the end of the telecast, Donahue was plugging the book, and he mistakenly said that *both* recipes prepared on the show were in the cookbook.

A few days later at the firehouse, our regular mailman stopped in and said he had some mail for us, probably about the cookbook. Well, he proceeds to carry in two of those large gray sacks filled with over 2,000 letters from Donahue viewers who wanted the crab rollup recipe! Needless to say, we had inserts made up of this recipe to put into future printings of the cookbook.

Danny Prince

CRAB ROLLUPS

SERVINGS: 60

1 stick (½ cup) butter
8 ounces Velveeta cheese
1 small can crabmeat (drained and picked over for shells)
20 slices white bread (such as Wonder), crusts removed, flattened with a rolling
  pin
½ cup melted butter
½ cup sesame seeds, or as needed

Stirring, melt the butter and Velveeta cheese in the top of a double boiler over simmering water. When the butter and cheese are melted and smooth, add the crabmeat and mix. When the mixture's a spreadable consistency, spread like peanut butter on the thinned slices of bread. Roll up each slice like a jelly roll. Dip each roll in melted butter and roll in sesame seeds. Place the rolled bread slices on a cookie sheet, seam side down. Freeze.

When ready to serve, preheat the oven to 350° F.

Cut each roll into thirds. Bake until golden brown, approximately 10 minutes.

Danny Prince
Ladder 156, F.D.N.Y.

CRAB-STUFFED MUSHROOMS

SERVINGS: 12–15

3 dozen large fresh mushrooms
1 can (7½ ounces) crabmeat, drained and flaked
1 tablespoon snipped fresh parsley
1 tablespoon chopped pimiento
1 teaspoon chopped capers
1 teaspoon dry mustard
½ cup mayonnaise

Preheat the oven to 375° F.

Wash and dry the mushrooms; remove stems. Combine the crabmeat, parsley, pimiento, capers, and chopped mushroom stems. Blend the mustard and mayonnaise, toss with the crabmeat mixture. Fill the mushroom caps with the mixture and bake for 10 minutes.

Joe Ginley, retired
Engine 8, F.D.N.Y.

ZUCCHINI APPETIZER

SERVINGS: 8

3 cups shredded zucchini
1 cup Bisquick
½ cup chopped onion
½ cup grated Parmesan cheese
2 tablespoons chopped fresh parsley
½ teaspoon salt
1 teaspoon Italian seasoning
½ teaspoon dried oregano or marjoram
½ cup vegetable oil
Pepper to taste
4 eggs, beaten
1 garlic clove, chopped

Preheat the oven to 350° F.

Combine all the ingredients in a bowl. Spread in a greased 13 x 9 x 2-inch pan and bake for 35 minutes until golden brown.

Serve warm.

Mrs. Shirley Reed
Secretary to the Fire Commissioner, F.D.N.Y.

SCUNGILLI (CONCH) SALAD

SERVINGS: 4–6

4 cans (8 ounces each) scungilli
1 garlic clove, coarsely chopped
⅓ cup vegetable oil
⅓ cup lemon juice
1 tablespoon dried oregano
1 tablespoon dried basil
1 tablespoon dried parsley
Black pepper

Rinse the scungilli with cold water, drain, and put in a large jar. Add the garlic, oil, lemon juice, oregano, basil, and parsley. Sprinkle with black pepper. Close the jar tightly; shake well. Put in the refrigerator and shake occasionally. The longer it stays, the sharper the taste. Serve *whenever.*

VARIATION: Squid salad is prepared in much the same way. Before adding to the jar, boil 8 large, cleaned squid in water for 2 to 3 minutes. Cut into bite-size pieces, then proceed as above.

John Sineno, retired
Engine 58, F.D.N.Y.

BORO-WIDE CHICKEN SOUP

In cold weather the guys always want me to make soup. Now this recipe has fed up to 20 big guys at one sitting, but it can be kept and reheated when you feel that cold coming on. Incidentally, none of my crew has been out with a winter cold in seven years.

SERVINGS: 16–20

4 nice chickens in a big pot of boiling water, with herbs and spices already in
Stalk of celery with 2 large onions quartered; add to the chicken pot
3 bags of fresh carrots, cut in 1-inch pieces
4 potatoes, diced (for the Irish guys)
A parsnip or two
3 bags frozen mixed vegetables (need the vitamins)
2 packages mushrooms, sliced (but only because the captain hated them)
2 pounds of Ditalini or other macaroni, cooked and put in the bowls just before
   the soup

What I do is boil the chicken for about 45 minutes until it slides off the bones; cook the carrots, potatoes, and parsnips on the side. When the chicken is done, have the guys peel the meat off in chunks. While this is being done, add the cooked veggies, frozen mixed vegetables, and mushrooms to the broth. By the time the chicken is peeled, the soup will be done.

Serve with plenty of grated cheese and lots of Italian bread.

John D'Attore
Engine 66, F.D.N.Y.

CHICKEN RICE SOUP

SERVINGS: 6–8

1 whole chicken, cut up
1 tablespoon chopped fresh parsley
4 large carrots, peeled and diced
2 cups long-grain white rice
2 chicken bouillon cubes
Grated Parmesan cheese to taste

Wash the chicken and put in a stockpot. Cover with water (approximately 6 cups) and add the parsley and carrots. Bring to a slow boil and cook until the chicken is done. When the chicken is cooked, remove from the pot, bone, and shred. To the liquid in the pot add the rice and bouillon cubes. Cover and cook until the rice is done. Add the shredded chicken and serve, garnished with Parmesan cheese.

John Sineno, retired
Engine 58, F.D.N.Y.

CHICKEN AND ESCAROLE SOUP

SERVINGS: 6–8 (DEPENDING UPON AMOUNT OF INGREDIENTS USED)

1 chicken, cut up
1 celery stalk, chopped
4 carrots, chopped
1 onion, chopped
Salt and pepper to taste
2 bunches escarole, washed and trimmed
1 pound ground meat (such as beef)
Chopped garlic
Bread crumbs
Cheese
Chopped fresh parsley

Cover the chicken with water, cover, and bring to a boil. Add the celery, carrots, onion, salt, and pepper. Reduce the heat and simmer till tender. Remove the chicken from the broth; strain the broth and return to the pot. When the chicken is cool enough to handle, remove the skin and bones and shred the meat. Set aside.

In a separate pot, boil the escarole for 20 to 30 minutes. Drain and let cool.

Season the ground meat with garlic, bread crumbs, cheese, and parsley, to taste. Mold the mixture into small meatballs, the size of dimes. Add the meatballs, escarole, and shredded chicken to the simmering broth. Cook for an additional 15 to 20 minutes.

John Sineno, retired
Engine 58, F.D.N.Y.

The name came because it reminds me of the low tide at Garrison Beach.

SERVINGS: 12–16

6 large heads escarole
Plenty of garlic (the more the better, at least one head)
6 to 8 large cans kidney beans, both red and white
2 pounds elbow macaroni

Clean the escarole and chop coarsely.

Bring 4 quarts of water to a full boil in a large pot. Add the escarole. Cook 8 to 10 minutes on a low boil. Add the garlic and beans with their liquid, and cook 6 to 8 minutes.

Cook the elbow macaroni separately until al dente. Drain the elbows and add to the escarole.

Serve with meatloaf, sandwiches, hamburgers, etc.

Frankie Action Solimeno
41st Battalion, F.D.N.Y.

CARMELA'S SPECIAL BEAN SOUP

The soup can be poured over hard Italian biscuits or over Italian bread, and served with grated Parmesan cheese.

SERVINGS: 4

2 tablespoons of your favorite cooking oil
1 medium onion, diced
2 large garlic cloves, diced
½ pound chopped beef chuck
3 sausage links (hot or sweet, to taste)
1 16-ounce can Italian plum tomatoes, drained
3 celery stalks, cut into chunks
Salt and pepper to taste
4 cups water
1 large can cannellini beans
1 cup small elbow macaroni

Heat the cooking oil in a 2-quart saucepan. Add the onion and garlic and sauté lightly. Remove from the oil and set aside. Add the chopped meat to the pan and brown; remove and set aside. Brown the sausage links and remove; cut into bite-size chunks and set aside.

Pour the strained tomatoes into the oil, stirring gently, and let simmer for 10 minutes. Add the celery and cook another 5 minutes. Return all the cooked ingredients to the pan, stirring to let the meats absorb the sauce. Cook, covered, for 1 hour. Add seasoning to taste. Pour in the water and add the beans; cook, covered, for an additional ½ hour.

Meanwhile, cook the elbow macaroni according to package directions. When the soup is done, add the cooked macaroni and stir. Serve immediately.

Carmela Rosseno Ciance
District Office 12, F.D.N.Y.

FIREHOUSE BEAN SOUP

SERVINGS: 12

4 pounds dried Great Northern or navy beans
1 smoked ham (6 pounds), rubbed with ground cloves and sprinkled with brown
  sugar
10 quarts water
5 pounds potatoes, peeled and diced
2 large onions, chopped
4 bay leaves
2 large cans whole tomatoes
Salt and pepper to taste

Soak the beans in water to cover overnight. Also the night before, bake the ham.

Drain the beans in the morning and cut the ham off the bone and cut in small pieces. Add the water to the beans in the pot and cook for 1–1½ hours before adding the other ingredients, then add the diced potatoes, onions, bay leaves, and ham and bone. Cook until the potatoes are done but still firm. Add the tomatoes and cook 30 more minutes. Season to your own taste. Keep a check on the water. More may need to be added as the soup cooks.

Richard S. Smith
Randallstown Station #18, Westminster, Maryland

SERVINGS: 8

1¼ cup dried pinto beans, rinsed
5 cups water
3 slices bacon, chopped
2 medium onions, finely chopped
2 garlic cloves, minced
1 can (16 ounces) tomatoes, cut up
1½ cups brown rice, cooked
2 teaspoons salt
½ teaspoon paprika
¼ teaspoon pepper

Combine the beans and 3 cups of the water in a 5–6-quart kettle or Dutch oven. Cover, let stand overnight or bring to a boil, reduce the heat, and let simmer 2 minutes. Let stand 1 hour. Do not drain. Simmer, covered, for 2 hours, or until the beans are tender. Drain, reserving 2 cups of liquid.

Cook the bacon in the Dutch oven until almost crisp. Add the onion and garlic. Cook and stir until the vegetables are tender but not brown. Stir in the cooked pinto beans, tomatoes, rice, salt, paprika, and pepper. Add the reserved bean liquid and remaining 2 cups water. Bring the mixture to a boil. Reduce the heat, cover, and simmer 1 hour, stirring occasionally If the soup is too thick, add water.

Don Schwerdt
Engine 4, Springfield, New Jersey

BEEF BARLEY VEGETABLE SOUP

Serve this soup with biscuits and green salad.

SERVINGS: ENOUGH FOR AT LEAST 6 HEARTY APPETITES

1½ to 2 pounds boneless beef, cut into ½-inch cubes
2 tablespoons margarine
1 medium onion, chopped
2 celery stalks, chopped
1 tablespoon chopped fresh parsley
Salt and pepper to taste
1 can (28 ounces) tomatoes, broken up
1 can (16 ounces) tomatoes, broken up
¾ cup barley
1 bag (16 ounces) frozen mixed vegetables (corn, peas, lima beans, green beans)

Brown the beef slightly, in the margarine, in a large saucepan. Add the onion, celery, parsley, salt and pepper, and water to cover. Simmer 1 to 1½ hours, covered. Add the tomatoes and bring to a boil. Add the barley and cook, covered, 45 minutes, stirring occasionally to keep the barley from sticking to the bottom. Add the frozen vegetables. Simmer on medium heat for 45 minutes, or until the vegetables are cooked to your desired tenderness.

Warren G. Kessler, retired
Engine 268, F.D.N.Y.
Charlene A. Kessler, Ladies Auxiliary Volunteer
Fire Department, Clarksville, Virginia

GOULASH SOUP

Here's another spicy beauty. This is great with a fresh loaf of pumpernickel or rye bread.

A whole chili may heat this soup more than you like—you could use a dash of red pepper instead.

SERVINGS: 6–8

2 tablespoons vegetable oil
4 pounds boneless beef chuck, cut into ½-inch cubes
3 tablespoons butter
3 large onions, chopped
3 large garlic cloves, minced
¼ cup all-purpose flour
2 quarts beef stock, homemade or canned (if canned, omit salt called for in
  recipe)
1 tablespoon sweet Hungarian paprika (domestic, if you must)
2 large green peppers, cut into narrow strips
1 tablespoon salt
½ teaspoon or more freshly ground pepper
1 heaping teaspoon caraway seeds
1 can (16 ounces) tomatoes and liquid, chopped
1 small dried red chili pepper, crushed
2 medium potatoes, peeled and cut into eighths
Sour cream (optional; purists don't use it—tastes good though)

Heat the oil in a large saucepan over medium-high heat and brown the meat well. Reduce the heat to medium. Add the butter and melt, add the onions and garlic and sauté 5 minutes.

Dissolve the flour well in some of the stock (Wondra flour dissolves easiest). Add to the saucepan. Stir in the paprika, rest of the stock, green peppers, salt, pepper, caraway seed, tomatoes, and chili. Cover, bring to a boil, reduce the heat, and simmer 2 hours.

Add the potatoes and simmer 20 minutes or until the potatoes are tender. Garnish with sour cream, if you wish, and serve.

NOTE: Like chilies and stews, this dish is best made a day ahead. Complete through the next-to-last step. Refrigerate overnight, skim off the fat, reheat, then add the potatoes as above.

William J. White, retired
Ladder 26 and 164

SERVINGS: 16-20

2 gallons water
6 beef bouillon cubes
6 chicken bouillon cubes
1 package soup greens, finely chopped
Pepper to taste
Garlic powder to taste
2 pounds ground beef
1 large head escarole, rinsed and chopped
2 packages (10 ounces each) fresh spinach, rinsed and chopped
2 pounds tortellini
1 egg, beaten
2 tablespoons chopped fresh parsley
2 tablespoons Worcestershire sauce

Into a large soup pot put the water, beef and chicken bouillon cubes, soup greens, pepper, and garlic powder. Simmer for 1 hour.

Form the beef into meatballs. After the soup has simmered for 1 hour, add the meatballs, escarole, spinach, and tortellini. Simmer till the meatballs are thoroughly cooked. Add the egg and parsley. Five minutes before serving, add the Worcestershire sauce.

Capt. Pat Buttino
Engine 263, F.D.N.Y.

TURKEY ALBONDIGAS SOUP

At the firehouse I serve this soup with warm tortillas or good bread, and provide garnishes of minced fresh cilantro, leaf oregano, lime or lemon wedges.

SERVINGS: GENEROUS 10 (OR ENOUGH FOR 6 HUNGRY FIREFIGHTERS)

Soup:
1 can (28 ounces) tomatoes, undrained and coarsely chopped
2 quarts water
2 celery stalks, sliced, about 2 cups
4 or 5 carrots, sliced, about 3 cups
1 medium onion, chopped
1 garlic clove, finely minced
1 can (4 ounces) mild peeled chilies, drained and cut in ¼-inch strips
⅓ can El Paso brand hot tomato sauce (reserve remaining sauce for those who
   like it hotter)
1 teaspoon seasoned salt
Dash of black pepper, to taste
3 large potatoes
1 can (30 ounces) hominy, drained

Meatballs:
2 pounds ground turkey
1 egg
1 teaspoon seasoned salt
1 cup seasoned bread crumbs

In an 8-quart soup pot bring the tomatoes, water, celery, carrots, onion, garlic, chilies, El Paso sauce, salt and pepper to a boil. While waiting for the boil, peel and quarter the potatoes lengthwise and cut into ¼-inch slices to make about 6 cups. Add the potatoes and continue cooking for 30 minutes.

Mix the ground turkey, egg, seasoned salt, and seasoned bread crumbs. Shape into 1¼-inch meatballs.

When the carrots and potatoes are tender, stir in hominy, then the meatballs, stirring gently. Bring back to the boil, then reduce the heat and simmer 30 minutes more.

Tyre N. Wood
Fire Department, Whittier, California

VEGETABLE SOUP EXPRESS

(A 6-Man Firehouse Delight)

SERVINGS: ENOUGH FOR 6 HUNGRY FIREMEN

6 medium onions, chopped
6 celery stalks, chopped
3 sprigs parsley, finely chopped
1 bay leaf
3 tablespoons butter
8 large tomatoes, pureed
8 carrots, peeled and diced
1 pound string beans, diced
6 medium potatoes, peeled and cut into large cubes
3 quarts water, or as needed
8 beef bouillon cubes
⅛ teaspoon pepper
Salt to taste

In a 10-quart pot, sauté the onions, celery, parsley, and bay leaf in the butter. Add water as needed in ¼-cup amounts for 20 minutes. In a 5-quart pot combine the tomatoes, carrots, string beans, potatoes, and 2 quarts of the water. Cook over a medium flame for 15 minutes, then over a low flame for an additional 5 minutes. Pour the vegetable mixture into the 10-quart pot. Add another quart water and the bouillon cubes. Bring to a low boil with a lid and cook for 30 minutes. Add the pepper and salt to taste.

J. d'Emic
Engine 248, F.D.N.Y.

POTATO SOUP

SERVINGS: 12

3 pounds beef soup bones, cracked
3 medium potatoes, peeled and cut in large pieces
4 medium carrots, peeled and cut in large pieces
2 medium turnips, peeled and coarsely chopped
2 medium onions, cut in quarters
⅓ cup snipped fresh parsley
3 tablespoons butter
3 quarts water
4 teaspoons salt
1 cup half-and-half
2 egg yolks, beaten
Grated Parmesan cheese
Additional snipped parsley

Place the soup bones in a large baking pan. Bake in a preheated 450° F oven 15 to 20 minutes, or until browned. In a large kettle, sauté the potatoes, carrots, turnips, onions, and ⅓ cup snipped parsley in the butter until slightly browned. Add the water, salt, and browned soup bones. Cover and simmer over low heat for about 1 hour.

Remove any meat from the bones, and discard the bones. Strain the soup, reserving stock and vegetables. Place the vegetables in a blender and puree, or force through a fine sieve. Mix together the stock, pieces of meat, and pureed vegetables. Bring to a boil and gently boil until the soup reduces to 2½ quarts. Before serving, heat the soup. Combine the half-and-half and beaten egg yolks. Stir a small amount of soup into the egg mixture, and return to the soup. Heat until slightly thick. Serve with a sprinkle of Parmesan cheese and additional snipped parsley.

Don Schwerdt
Engine 4, Springfield, New Jersey

NEW YORK CLAM CHOWDER

SERVINGS: 6

¼ pound bacon, chopped
1 onion, chopped
1 can (16 ounces) whole tomatoes, undrained
½ teaspoon salt
¼ teaspoon pepper
1 carrot, peeled and sliced
1 cup peeled and cubed potatoes
2 cups hot water
1 dozen large clams, chopped, with their juice (must be hard clams)
1 teaspoon dried thyme

Brown the bacon with the onion in a large saucepan. When the onion is soft, add the tomatoes, salt, pepper, carrot, potatoes, and water. Bring to a boil, then cook until the potatoes and carrots are tender. Add the clams, thyme, and clam juice. Simmer for 5 minutes longer.

Fireman Tom Stack
Brooklyn/Queens Holy Name Society

MAXIE PEARL'S CHOWDER

(Manhattan Style)

SERVINGS: 8 (YIELDS 20 CUPS)

6 slices bacon (optional)
4 stalks celery, sliced across at ¼-inch intervals
½ large bell pepper, chopped
2 carrots, washed, not peeled, and sliced into ¼-inch disks
1 large Spanish onion, diced
10 cups water
3 dozen or more unshucked standard oysters, shells scrubbed
1 large red potato, peeled and cut into ½-inch cubes
2 cups canned tomato puree
1 can (28 ounces) whole tomatoes, undrained and chopped
½ cup dry red wine
¼ cup finely chopped fresh parsley
1½ teaspoons pepper
1 tablespoon sugar
½ teaspoon dried oregano
1 bay leaf
Salt to taste

In a large stockpot over moderate heat, cook the bacon until crisp. Remove the bacon with a slotted spoon, blot with paper towels, crumble, and refrigerate. Drain all but 2 tablespoons of bacon grease from the stockpot. If you elect not to use bacon, replace those 2 tablespoons of rendered fat with an equivalent amount of vegetable oil, butter, or margarine.

Add the celery, bell pepper, carrots, and onion to the fat. Sauté until the onion is translucent.

In a separate pot, combine the water and oysters. Cover and boil between a period of 15 and 20 minutes. Remove the oysters and permit them to cool. Discard those that have not opened, as they were deceased prior to the final plunge that deprived their fellow bivalves of a full life, are laden with sand, or perhaps encase a pearl. (If curiosity gets the better of you, open them and check.) Through a coffee filter placed in a sieve, strain the oyster liquor into the stockpot, changing the filter as necessary. Extract the oyster meat and incorporate it, along with the remaining ingredients and the reserved crumbled bacon, if using, into the pot. Simmer, uncovered, for 1½ hours. Stir periodically.

Ladle the chowder into bowls or a tureen. Crown with additional bits of crumbled bacon.

Warren William Kessler
Warren G. Kessler, retired
Engine 268, F.D.N.Y.

SERVINGS: 6

¼ cup chopped bacon or salt pork
½ cup chopped onion
2 cups boiling water
1 can (16 ounces) whole tomatoes, undrained
1 cup peeled and diced potatoes
½ cup peeled and diced carrot
½ cup chopped celery
¼ cup ketchup
1 tablespoon Worcestershire sauce
1 teaspoon salt
¼ teaspoon dried thyme
1 pound fish fillets, cut into 1-inch pieces
Chopped fresh parsley

Fry the bacon until crisp in a large saucepan. Add the onion and cook until tender. Add the water, tomatoes, potatoes, carrot, celery, ketchup, and seasonings. Cover and simmer 45 minutes until the vegetables are tender. Add the fish. Cover and simmer about 10 minutes, until the fish flakes easily with a fork. Sprinkle with parsley and serve.

Don Schwerdt
Engine 4, Springfield, New Jersey

Pastas

Plain Marinara Sauce/*Sineno*

Pasta with Olive Oil and Garlic Sauce "My Way"/*Ubertini*

Accidental Sauce/*Sineno and Prince*

Pesto Sauce/*Bruno*

Wild Irish "Rouge"/*McLaughlin*

Pasta with Sardines, Palermo Style/*Vinci*

Linguine with Clam Sauce/*Shea*

Joe Lo's Green Fettuccine with Sauce/*Losinno*

White Fish Sauce over Fettuccine/*Sineno*

Shrimp and Sun-Dried Tomatoes/*Prince*

Rigatoni with Chicken/*Donahue*

Philippine-Style Spaghetti/*Angelone*

Chicken and Broccoli Stir-Fry Over Pan-Fried Noodles/
Sineno and Marazzo

Pasta e Fagioli/*Luizzi*

Basta Pasta (Neapolitan Style)/*de Meo*

Cavatelli and Broccoli/*Dipippo*

Pasta Belmontese/*Mancusi*

Pasta Lucia/*Monte*

Rigatoni all'Amatriciana/*Triozzi*

Pasta with Walnuts, Parsley, and Parmesan Cheese/*Monte*

Baked Macaroni/*Sineno*

Pastitso (Greek Baked Macaroni)/*Lomuscio*

Manicotti/*Prince*

Fire Commissioner's Fettuccine/*Spinnato*

Spinach Lasagne Rolls/*Wilkerson*

Pasta 202/*Mancusi*

Fettuccine alla Tuscolana II/*Driusi*

PLAIN MARINARA SAUCE
(BASIC SAUCE)

This basic sauce can be modified for a variety of dishes by adding different spices and meats.

SERVINGS: 6–7 QUARTS

2-gallon can crushed tomatoes
Salt and pepper
2 tablespoons chopped fresh basil
1 teaspoon dried mint
1 bunch parsley, finely chopped
1 stick (½ cup) margarine
½ cup olive oil
7 garlic cloves, chopped
1 onion, chopped
3 carrots, peeled and chopped
1 cup dry white wine

Bring the crushed tomatoes to a boil in a large pot. Reduce the heat to a simmer and add salt and pepper to taste, chopped basil, mint, and parsley. Let simmer, uncovered, for 1 hour.

Heat the margarine and olive oil in a frying pan. Add the garlic, onion, and carrots. Let simmer till brown. Remove and discard the carrots. Add the wine; simmer till it boils. Put the mixture through a strainer into the tomato sauce. Discard garlic and onion remains. Add salt and pepper to taste.

John Sineno, retired
Engine 58, F.D.N.Y.

PASTA WITH OLIVE OIL AND GARLIC SAUCE "MY WAY"

SERVINGS: 11

5 pounds sausage (hot/sweet or combo)
5 bunches of broccoli, quartered
5 pounds pasta (any type)
1½ cups olive oil
1 teaspoon salt
6 garlic cloves, chopped
Garlic powder, onion powder, parsley flakes, dried basil, and pepper to taste
1 large chunk Locatelli cheese, grated

Preheat the oven to 350° F.

Bake the sausage in a large pan in the oven for approximately 1 hour, turning occasionally (split one side of sausage with knife to make sure it cooks through). Meanwhile, steam the broccoli for 40 minutes. Cook the pasta with a teaspoon of the olive oil and a teaspoon salt in a large pot.

Drain the pasta and place in a large bowl. Fry the garlic in the remaining oil in a large frying pan till the garlic is brown; then pour over the pasta. Quarter the cooked sausages and add to the pasta, along with the broccoli, garlic powder, onion powder, parsley flakes, basil, and pepper. Mix all together.

Serve with Locatelli cheese on the side for topping (Locatelli makes the meal!).

Thomas Ubertini
Engine 66, F.D.N.Y.

The Festival Cafe was preparing some dishes from the original cookbook for a promotion we were doing. I submitted two entries: artichoke pie and home-made manicotti. When I got to the dinner, I did see manicotti, but manicotti with a green sauce. Everyone said, "This is great—Here's one of the recipes that's going in the book." I said, "That's not mine—I submitted artichoke pie and my homemade manicotti."

What they'd done was combine the two recipes to get manicotti with arti-choke sauce—and that's why I called this Accidental Sauce!

SERVINGS: 2 CUPS OR MORE, DEPENDING ON DESIRED THICKNESS

2 cans (12 ounces each) artichoke hearts, drained and quartered
¼ teaspoon minced garlic
1 teaspoon chopped fresh parsley
1 tablespoon olive oil
¾ cup heavy cream
½ cup chicken stock or broth, or as necessary
2 tablespoons Parmesan cheese, grated

Put all the ingredients except the grated cheese in a saucepan. Simmer, cov-ered, for 30 minutes, then process in a food processor or blender until smooth. Press with a coarse strainer, then put back into saucepan, add the cheese, and heat. Add more chicken broth or stock if necessary to thin sauce.

Serve over chicken, pasta, or manicotti.

John Sineno, retired
Engine 58, F.D.N.Y.
Danny Prince
Ladder 156, F.D.N.Y.

PESTO SAUCE

Serve the pesto sauce at room temperature on hot cooked spaghetti or linguine. If desired, add more cheese or a little butter to the pesto and spaghetti, or even a little water to avoid dryness.

SERVINGS: 4

1 small bunch fresh basil
2 garlic cloves, peeled
2 tablespoons olive oil
2 tablespoons grated Parmesan cheese

Wash the basil thoroughly and remove the stems. Dry well. Place the ingredients in a blender or food processor. Blend until well chopped; be sure not to liquefy. Store the sauce in a well-sealed jar, covered with a layer of olive oil.

First Deputy Fire Commissioner Joseph Bruno
F.D.N.Y.

Firefighting Family

On "Why they call me Mama . . ."

It's been said I make sure everyone else sits down and eats, and only then do I eat.

When I first walked in the firehouse I was a "brother." From brother I made it to "Mama," specifically "Mama Sineno's Kitchen." And then Danny Prince started calling me "Papa," and I became in charge of the whole "family."

John Sineno

WILD IRISH "ROUGE"

(A Pasta Mélange)

SERVINGS: 3–4

Pinch of salt
Olive oil
1 pound spaghetti (preferably thin)
5 strips bacon
1 large garlic clove, crushed
1 stick (½ cup) margarine or butter
1 can (16 ounces) sauerkraut, drained
1 can (4 ounces) sliced mushrooms, drained
Caraway seeds
Coarse pepper
1 jar (7 ounces) sliced pimientos, drained
4 tablespoons grated Parmesan cheese
Chopped fresh parsley

Bring 3 quarts water to a boil with a pinch of salt and 4 tablespoons olive oil. Add spaghetti and boil for about 11 minutes.

Meanwhile, fry the bacon, crumble, and return to the bacon grease in the frying pan. Add the garlic, margarine, 3 tablespoons olive oil, sauerkraut, mushrooms, and a pinch each of caraway seeds and coarse pepper. Sauté, tossing frequently; do not burn.

Put the pimientos and 2 tablespoons oil in a small pot, but do not heat until the spaghetti is drained and in a warm bowl. Add the sauerkraut mixture to the spaghetti. Toss. Garnish with grated cheese, sprinkle with parsley, and pour the heated pimientos over.

Battalion Chief Jack "Black Jack" McLaughlin, retired
53rd Battalion, F.D.N.Y.

PASTA WITH SARDINES, PALERMO STYLE

(From Sicily with Love)

SERVINGS: 4

2 cups leaf tops from fennel (if unavailable, use 1 tablespoon fennel seeds
  wrapped in cheesecloth)
½ cup olive oil
2 tablespoons chopped onion
4 flat anchovy fillets, chopped
⅓ cup pignoli nuts
1 tablespoon raisins, soaked in cold water for 15 minutes
1½ tablespoons tomato paste
½ package saffron threads, dissolved in 1 cup water
Salt and pepper to taste
3 cans (3¾ ounces each) boneless sardines packed in olive oil, drained
1 pound bucatini or perciatelli macaroni (imported from Italy)
½ cup unseasoned bread crumbs, lightly toasted in the oven

Wash the fennel tops in cold water. Bring 4 to 5 quarts of water to boil in the pot that you will use to cook the pasta. Cook the tops for about 10 minutes. Turn off the heat and remove the greens; do not discard the water. Do the same if using fennel seeds. Gently squeeze the moisture out of the greens and chop.

Choose a pan large enough to contain all the ingredients except the pasta. Put in the olive oil, onion, and anchovies. Heat over a medium flame, stirring occasionally. When the onion becomes translucent, put in the chopped fennel and cook for 5 to 6 minutes. Add the pignoli, raisins, tomato paste, and dissolved saffron. Add salt and pepper. Cook on medium heat until the water in the pan has bubbled away completely. Put in the sardines, turn them for a few seconds, and then turn off the heat.

Cook the pasta al dente. When the pasta is almost cooked, begin to heat the sauce over low heat. Place the pasta in a warm bowl, add the sauce and bread crumbs, toss thoroughly, and let the mixture rest a few minutes before serving.

Rev. Guy Vinci
Fire Department Chaplain, F.D.N.Y.

SERVINGS: 3–4

2 cans (7½ ounces each) whole baby clams, or 2 cups minced fresh clams
¼ cup plus 3 tablespoons olive oil or salad oil
½ stick (¼ cup) butter or margarine
3 large garlic cloves, minced
¾ cup Doxsee clam juice (optional)
2 tablespoons chopped fresh parsley
1½ teaspoons salt
8 ounces linguine
Parmesan cheese, grated

Drain canned clams if using, reserving ¾ cup of liquid; set aside. Slowly heat the ¼ cup oil and the butter in a skillet. Add the garlic and sauté until golden. Do not let the garlic brown. Remove the skillet from the heat. Stir in the clam liquid (Doxsee clam juice if using fresh clams), chopped parsley, and ½ teaspoon salt. Bring to a boil, reduce the heat, and simmer uncovered for 10 minutes.

While the mixture is simmering, boil the linguine till al dente (chewy) in 3 quarts water with remaining 1 teaspoon salt and the 3 tablespoons olive oil.

Add the clams to the skillet after the mixture has finished simmering. When the linguine is cooked, drain and place in a bowl. Pour in the contents of skillet, sprinkle with cheese, and toss.

Lt. J. Shea
Brooklyn/Queens Holy Name Society

JOE LO'S GREEN FETTUCCINE WITH SAUCE

Most firemen could stand to lose a few pounds. That's because most of their activity takes place around the firehouse kitchen—eating, talking about "jobs," etc., so this recipe is a quick one when time has gotten away from you. It helps if you're trying to eliminate that "firehouse bulge." The tuna fish in the recipe actually tastes like chicken.

SERVINGS: 4

3 garlic cloves, chopped
¼ cup olive oil
1 can (7½ ounces) tuna, drained
½ cup green olives with pimientos, sliced in half
1 large can crushed Italian tomatoes
2 tablespoons chopped fresh parsley
1 teaspoon dried oregano
½ teaspoon crushed red pepper
1 to 1½ pounds green fettuccine, cooked

Sauté the garlic in the oil in a large saucepan. Add everything else except the fettuccine and cook 5 to 10 minutes. Serve over the green fettuccine.

Joe Losinno
Engine 302, F.D.N.Y.

WHITE FISH SAUCE OVER FETTUCCINE

This is also a big hit over rice—the way my son Thomas always loved it. Enjoy!

SERVINGS: 8–12

1 stick (½ cup) margarine
¼ teaspoon granulated garlic
1 tablespoon parsley flakes
1 tablespoon dried basil
1 cup all-purpose flour
2 quarts half-and-half or milk
6 to 8 ounces Italian cheese (according to your taste), grated
Pinch of black pepper
1 pound imitation or real crabmeat
1 pound small shrimp, shelled and deveined
1 pound small scallops
2 to 3 pounds fettuccine or noodles, cooked

Melt the margarine in a deep frying pan. Add garlic, parsley, basil, and flour, and blend well together. Add one quart of the half-and-half (or milk). Simmer for a bit, stirring. Add the other quart of half-and-half (or milk), and simmer until it blends. Add the grated cheese and black pepper. Simmer according to taste and consistency—if too thick add more milk; if too thin, add more flour. Add crabmeat, shrimp, and scallops. When the scallops are cooked, the sauce is done—it's a very quick sauce.

Serve over the fettuccine.

John Sineno, retired
Engine 58, F.D.N.Y.

SHRIMP AND SUN-DRIED TOMATOES

SERVINGS: 6

2 pounds medium shrimp, shelled and deveined, shells reserved
1 cup water
2 to 3 garlic cloves
¼ cup vegetable oil
4 ounces loose sun-dried tomatoes
1 teaspoon dried basil, or to taste
2 pounds your choice of pasta, linguine, spaghetti, etc.

Place the shrimp shells and water in a saucepan and simmer, covered, for 30 minutes. Drain, discard the shells, and reserve the liquid.

In a large skillet, sauté the shrimp with the garlic in the oil until pink. Add the sun-dried tomatoes, basil, and a bit of stock from the shrimp shells.

Prepare the pasta according to the directions on the box. Add the remaining stock to the shrimp mixture, pour over the pasta, and serve.

Danny Prince
Ladder 156, F.D.N.Y.

RIGATONI WITH CHICKEN

SERVINGS: 4

4 skinless, boneless chicken breast halves, sliced
½ cup oil-packed sun-dried tomatoes, drained and oil reserved
3 tablespoons chopped shallots
1 cup sliced black olives
2 tablespoons chopped garlic
1 cup dry (white) vermouth
½ stick (¼ cup) butter
½ cup chopped fresh basil
Salt and pepper to taste
1 pound rigatoni, cooked

Sauté the chicken in the sun-dried tomato oil in a large skillet, then remove from the pan.

Add the chopped shallots, olives, garlic, and sun-dried tomato. Cook 2 minutes, stirring frequently.

Return the chicken to the pan. Add the vermouth and cover. Let simmer 1 to 2 minutes.

Add the butter and basil and mix until the butter is incorporated. Add salt and pepper.

Add the rigatoni, mix, and serve hot.

Danny Donahue
Viper's Nest, Ladder 155, F.D.N.Y.

PHILIPPINE-STYLE SPAGHETTI

SERVINGS: 4

1 garlic clove, chopped
2 tablespoons vegetable oil
2 skinless, boneless chicken breast halves, boiled and shredded
8 small shrimp, shelled, deveined, and chopped
1 pork chop, broiled and shredded
1 carrot, peeled and finely shredded
½ cup finely shredded cabbage
4 ounces fresh mushrooms, chopped
1 pound #8 spaghetti or Philippine rice noodles, cooked
2 tablespoons soy sauce
½ teaspoon salt
Pepper

Sauté the garlic in the oil in a wok or skillet. Add the chicken, shrimp, and pork and cook, stirring frequently, until the shrimp is cooked. Add the carrot, cabbage, and mushrooms. Mix thoroughly, and just cook until tender (don't overcook). Stir in the cooked spaghetti or noodles until well blended. Add the soy sauce, salt, and pepper to taste. Cook and stir until well mixed.

Mike Angelone, retired
Engine 8, F.D.N.Y.

CHICKEN AND BROCCOLI STIR-FRY OVER PAN-FRIED NOODLES

SERVINGS: 6

Salt
8 ounces Oriental noodles
8 tablespoons vegetable oil
¼ cup soy sauce
¼ cup chicken broth
2 tablespoons cornstarch
1½ pounds boneless, skinless chicken breasts, cut into 1-inch medallions
1 bunch fresh broccoli, cut into 1-inch pieces
1 medium onion, quartered

In a saucepan bring 3 quarts of salted water to a boil and add noodles. Boil for 10 minutes. Remove and drain.

Heat 2 tablespoons of the oil in a wok or skillet over a medium flame. Add the noodles and let brown on each side, approximately 12 minutes per side. When you turn the noodles over, add another 2 tablespoons oil before browning other side. Remove and put in a serving dish.

Add 2 more tablespoons oil to the wok and heat on a medium flame. While heating the wok, in a small bowl combine the soy sauce, broth, and cornstarch, and mix till smooth. Set aside.

Add the chicken to the wok, stir-fry for 2 minutes, and remove. Add the broccoli and onion to the wok with the remaining 2 tablespoons oil and stir-fry 2 minutes. Add the chicken and sauce and stir-fry 4 minutes till the sauce is thickened. Remove from the heat and pour over the noodles.

John Sineno, retired
Engine 58, F.D.N.Y.
Jerrilynn Sineno Marazzo

PASTA E FAGIOLI

This recipe is a derivative of an old, tried, and proven recipe from the old days in Engine 314, when Joe Prinz was the keeper of the stove. On his last tour, sometime in 1989, he shared his culinary know-how with a few fortunate members lucky enough to be working that 9 x 6 tour with him. While we have made a few slight changes, the basic recipe remains the same—although we can't keep the price down to a measly $1.15 per man, as Joe could!

SERVINGS: 10–12

4 garlic cloves, minced
1 cup olive oil
5 large onions, coarsely chopped
2 cans (19 ounces each) cannellini beans (white kidney beans)
Salt and pepper to taste
Dried oregano, basil, and parsley to taste
Hot pepper sauce
8 cups canned chicken broth
1 head cabbage
1 head escarole, rinsed and trimmed
1 can (19 ounces) red kidney beans, undrained
1 can (19 ounces) chickpeas, undrained
1 pound elbow macaroni or small shell pasta
Grated Parmesan cheese

In a large pot, brown the garlic in the olive oil. When the garlic is browned, add the onions, 1 can of the cannellini beans, salt and pepper, oregano (quite a bit), basil, parsley, and a little hot sauce. Sauté over low-medium heat approximately 10 minutes.

In a separate pot, bring the chicken broth to a boil. Have the cabbage and escarole cut up into bite-size pieces and put them in the pot with the onions and beans. Immediately pour in the boiling chicken broth. Cover until the cabbage and escarole shrink down into the liquid. Simmer on low-medium heat approximately 45 minutes.

Add the remaining beans (cannellini, red kidney beans, and chickpeas), with liquid, and cook approximately another 30 minutes. In another separate pot, cook the pasta al dente and then add to the pot with the beans and vegetables.

Serve with plenty of grated cheese and hot sauce.

Danny Luizzi
Engine 314, F.D.N.Y.

BASTA PASTA
(NEAPOLITAN STYLE)

SERVINGS: 4

2 garlic cloves, minced
2 tablespoons olive oil
2 to 3 cups leftover spaghetti sauce
1 large can cannellini beans (white kidney beans)
4 ounces spaghetti, cooked

Sauté the minced garlic in the oil in a large saucepan. Add 2 to 3 cups sauce, then the kidney beans. Add the cooked spaghetti, then cover and simmer for 5 minutes.

Joseph M. de Meo
Chief of Department, F.D.N.Y.

CAVATELLI AND BROCCOLI

SERVINGS: 4

4 garlic cloves, chopped
2 tablespoons olive oil
1 head broccoli, tough stems removed, chopped
2 cups chicken broth, or as needed
1 pound frozen cavatelli
½ stick (¼ cup) butter, cut up
Salt to taste
Pepper to taste (optional)
Grated Parmesan cheese

In a wok or frying pan, sauté the chopped garlic in the oil. Before it browns, add the chopped broccoli and stir-fry until al dente. Add broth to cover the broccoli and cook on a low flame until tender.

Meanwhile, cook the cavatelli till desired doneness. Drain and place on a long platter. Toss gently with the butter. Pour the broccoli over the cavatelli, season with salt and pepper, and top with cheese.

Serve piping hot.

Capt. Vincent Dipippo
Engine 83, F.D.N.Y.

PASTA BELMONTESE

From the region of the Bronx, province of Belmont, Deputy Fire Commissioner Leonard A. Mancusi brings you pasta Belmontese:

SERVINGS: 4

Salt
2 tablespoons chopped fresh basil
½ cup extra virgin olive oil
1 pound linguine
3 sun-dried tomatoes (cut in eighths)
2 tablespoons chopped fresh parsley
6 garlic cloves, quartered
2 tablespoons tomato paste
1 small eggplant, cubed (about ¾ cup)
5 medium-size plum tomatoes, quartered
Crushed black pepper to taste
Grated Locatelli cheese (a handful)
Bread crumbs (a handful)
8 medium-size fresh basil leaves, sliced lengthwise in quarters

Bring water to a boil in a large pot, add a handful of salt, 2 tablespoons chopped basil, and ¼ cup of the oil. Add the pasta and cook to taste. Drain, re-serving some of the cooking liquid.

In a small saucepan combine the remaining ¼ cup of oil, the sun-dried tomatoes, parsley, garlic, and tomato paste. Heat through and set aside.

Place the eggplant in a microwave dish and microwave for 2 to 3 minutes. Add to the pasta in a bowl along with the fresh tomatoes. Add the mixture from the saucepan, some of the pasta water, as well as the black pepper, cheese, bread crumbs, and sliced basil.

Deputy Fire Commissioner Leonard A. Mancusi
The Bronx, F.D.N.Y.

Make sure all the ingredients are drained well, otherwise the end result will be soupy. Also, fresh Italian bread and cold imported beer go great with this dish—unless you're at the firehouse (because there's no drinking).

This meal is a two-bowl max, or you will lose it on the stairs of a six-story-walk-up top-floor fire. And if you're at home and married or single, I call this my romance meal: soft lights, soft music, pasta al dente, and then?

SERVINGS: 4 AS A FIRST DISH

1 pound bowtie (farfalle), macaroni, or penne zita regate (imported)
½ cup imported olive oil
2 to 3 garlic cloves, minced
4 ounces shrimp (48 count), shelled, deveined, and cut in half
1 bunch fresh arugula or spinach, trimmed, washed, and torn into pieces
1 large ripe tomato or 4 plum tomatoes, cut into bite-size pieces
Red and black pepper to taste
Grated Romano cheese

Put a large pot of water on to boil for the pasta. When the water boils, add the pasta.

Meanwhile, heat the olive oil over a low flame in a large frying pan. Add the minced garlic and sauté 1 minute. Add the shrimp and sauté till pink on one side, then flip over. Add the arugula or spinach and sauté 1 minute. Add the tomato and sauté 1 minute.

When the pasta is cooked al dente, drain well and mix with the above ingredients.

Ted Monte
Tower Ladder 138, F.D.N.Y.

The wine that ideally accompanies this typical Roman dish is either Frascati or Colli Albani. The Romans eat this dish with bucatini (perciatelli) instead of rigatoni as well.

SERVINGS: 6–8

2 large cans Italian peeled tomatoes (preferably San Marzano)
12 ounces pancetta, sliced thickly (12 ounces if sliced thickly should amount to about 8 slices); Canadian bacon can be substituted for the pancetta if it is not available)
2 tablespoons olive oil
1 hot pepper
White wine (Frascati or Colli Albani)
2 pounds rigatoni
4 ounces pecorino Romano cheese, grated

Crush the peeled tomatoes and dice the slices of pancetta. In a deep skillet or pot, simmer the diced pancetta along with the olive oil and hot pepper in enough white wine to barely cover the pancetta and pepper. When some of the wine begins to evaporate, add the crushed tomatoes and stir. Maintain a medium flame and stir occasionally for 20 minutes, give or take.

While you make the gravy (or sauce, as it is sometimes erroneously referred to), you should put the water on for the pasta. When the water comes to a boil, put in the rigatoni; stir occasionally until al dente. Serve the gravy over the rigatoni with a blizzard of pecorino cheese.

Capt. Robert Triozzi
Fire Protection, U.S. Embassy, Rome, Italy

PASTA WITH WALNUTS, PARSLEY, AND PARMESAN CHEESE

SERVINGS: 4 AS A SIDE DISH

1 cup walnuts
1 pound bowtie pasta (farfalle) or fettuccine
½ cup olive oil
Coarse salt (optional)
Pepper to taste
½ cup minced fresh parsley
¼ cup grated Parmesan cheese

Toast the walnuts in a dry skillet till brown. Chop coarsely and set aside. Cook the pasta, drain, place in a warm bowl, and add the oil, salt, and pepper; toss to coat. Divide among four plates and top with the walnuts, parsley, and cheese.

Ted Monte
Tower Ladder 138, F.D.N.Y.

BAKED MACARONI

SERVINGS: 12–15

3 pounds elbow or ziti macaroni
5 cans mushroom soup
8 ounces sharp cheddar cheese, grated
8 ounces Parmesan cheese, grated
4 cans (4 ounces each) mushrooms (caps and stems), drained

Preheat the oven to 350° F.

Cook the macaroni and transfer to a large baking dish. Heat the soup, adding 1 can of water to each can of soup. Pour the soup, cheeses, and mushrooms into the baking dish and mix well. Bake for 25 to 30 minutes.

John Sineno, retired
Engine 58, F.D.N.Y.

If there's anything firemen love to do more than fight fires, it's to talk about fire, over a good meal.

We were in the kitchen swapping fire stories one night when Jerry O'Keefe asked me if I remembered a particular fire we had both been at.

"You remember, John, that job we had up the street about a year ago?"

"You mean the ravioli fire?" I asked.

"The *what* fire?" asked Jerry.

"The ravioli fire," I said. "I remember fires by what I cooked that day."

It wasn't long after that that I noticed the men gently pulling my leg by referring to fires from then on as "the London broil fire," "the chicken Cordon Bleu fire," etc.

If there's anything firemen love to do more than talk about fires, it's to pull my leg, and probably eat it if I cooked it!

John Sineno

PASTITSO
(GREEK BAKED MACARONI)

SERVINGS: 8

1 pound elbow macaroni
1 pound butter
1 pound ground beef
2 cans (6 ounces each) tomato paste
1 pound grating cheese, grated
6 eggs
1 quart whole milk

Cook the macaroni according to package directions.

Melt the butter in a large frying pan, close flame. Add the meat and then add tomato paste. Cook about 15 minutes, till the meat is brown.

Heat the oven to 350° F.

Drain the macaroni and put macaroni in 15½ x 10½ x 2¼-inch baking pan. Add the cheese and mix. Add the meat and mix.

Beat the eggs. Add warmed milk to the eggs, pour the mixture over the macaroni, and mix. Bake uncovered 1 hour, till golden brown.

Battalion Chief Frank Lomuscio

MANICOTTI

Crepes:
3 eggs
1 cup sifted all-purpose flour
1 cup club soda
Pinch of Salt

Filling:
8 ounces ricotta cheese
4 ounces mozzarella cheese, shredded
1 egg
4 ounces Parmesan cheese, grated
Salt and pepper to taste
Chopped fresh parsley

2 cups tomato sauce, or as needed (good with Accidental Sauce, too! See page 50.)

Beat the eggs well with a whisk or fork; gradually add the flour, blending thoroughly. Add the club soda and salt; continue stirring until the batter is smooth. Set in the refrigerator for 1 hour before cooking. (Be sure to stir mixture before using.) Heat a small cured crepe pan 6 inches in diameter. Add a couple of tablespoons of batter at a time, tilting the pan to cover the bottom. Cook on one side only until the batter is set. Do not brown. Transfer to wax paper; continue until all the batter is used.

Preheat the oven to 350° F.

Mix all the filling ingredients in a bowl. Place 2 tablespoons of filling on each crepe and roll up. Place the manicotti in one layer in a baking dish and cover with tomato sauce. Bake for 15 minutes, or until the manicotti are piping hot throughout.

Danny Prince
Ladder 156, F.D.N.Y.

FIRE COMMISSIONER'S FETTUCCINE

SERVINGS: 8

2 sticks (1 cup) butter
8 ounces prosciutto, thinly sliced and shredded
12 ounces fresh mushrooms, thinly sliced
3 cups heavy cream
½ cup grated Parmesan cheese
1 quart tomato sauce
2 pounds fettuccine

Melt one stick of the butter in a frying pan. Sauté prosciutto and mushrooms in the butter; set aside. Melt the remaining stick of butter in the cream in a medium saucepan over low flame; gradually add the grated cheese, stirring constantly. Cook until well blended and thick. Set aside. Cook the fettuccine; drain and return to the pot. Heat the tomato sauce; then ladle half of it into fettuccine and mix. Gradually add half the white sauce and stir till the fettuccine is well coated and a light orange color.

Dish the fettuccine into individual bowls. Sprinkle some of the prosciutto and mushrooms on each serving.

Commissioner Joseph Spinnato
F.D.N.Y

I once asked "Spooky" Adrian to taste the macaroni to see if it was done. Spooky picked up a strand, and I thought he was going to taste it. Instead, he threw the strand up to the ceiling. He said, "If it sticks, it's done."

It stuck.

John Sineno

SPINACH LASAGNE ROLLS

SERVINGS: 4

1 package (10 ounces) frozen chopped spinach
8 lasagne noodles
1 large onion, chopped
1 medium green bell pepper, chopped
2 cups sliced fresh mushrooms
2 garlic cloves, minced
1 can (16 ounces) tomatoes, cut up
½ teaspoon dried basil, crushed
1 can (8 ounces) tomato sauce
½ teaspoon sugar
¼ teaspoon black pepper
2 cups low-fat cottage cheese
½ cup grated Parmesan cheese
1 egg, beaten
⅛ teaspoon ground nutmeg

Cook the spinach and lasagne noodles separately according to package directions. Drain and set aside.

For the sauce, spray a large saucepan with cooking spray and heat over medium heat. Add the onion, green pepper, mushrooms, and garlic. Cook until the vegetables are tender. Stir the undrained tomatoes, basil, tomato sauce, sugar, and black pepper into the vegetables. Bring to a boil, then reduce the heat. Simmer, uncovered, 5 minutes, or until slightly thickened.

While the sauce is cooking, stir together the spinach, cottage cheese, Parmesan cheese, egg, and nutmeg.

Spoon 1 cup of the sauce mixture into a 12 x 7½ x 2-inch baking dish. Spread a scant ½ cup spinach mixture on each noodle. Roll up each noodle, jelly-roll style, beginning at one short end. Place the rolls, seam down, in the dish. Spoon on remaining sauce. If not serving immediately, cover with plastic wrap and refrigerate 2 to 24 hours.

Before serving, remove the plastic wrap. Cover with foil. Bake in a preheated 375° F oven for 40 to 45 minutes, or until bubbly.

Tony Wilkerson
Volunteer Fire Department, Clarksville, Virginia

SERVINGS: 4

Salt
½ cup extra virgin olive oil
1 pound ziti
5 tablespoons butter
¾ cup sun-dried tomatoes, seeded and chopped
¾ cup vodka
1 can (8 ounces) peeled tomatoes, drained, seeded, and chopped
¾ cup heavy cream
Freshly grated Parmesan cheese

Bring cold water to a boil in a large pot with a handful of salt and ¼ cup olive oil. Add the pasta and cook.

Heat the butter and remaining ¼ cup olive oil in a small saucepan. Add the sun-dried tomatoes and sauté for a few minutes. Add the vodka and let evaporate. Add the peeled tomatoes and bring to a boil. Reduce the heat, cover, and simmer about 10 minutes. Add the heavy cream, bring to a boil, and remove from the heat.

Drain the pasta, but reserve one cup of its cooking liquid. Put the pasta in a serving dish and add the sauce and some Parmesan cheese. Mix well; if the pasta looks dry, add a little of the pasta water.

Deputy Fire Commissioner Leonard A. Mancusi
The Bronx, F.D.N.Y.

FETTUCCINE ALLA TUSCOLANA II

This dish is a specialty of Shift "B" at Engine Company 12-A in the Tuscolana area on the south side of Rome when they work the night tour (8 P.M. to 8 A.M.) after having worked the day tour (8 A.M. to 8 P.M.) the day before. They serve this course when there is a little bit of "gravy" (or sauce) left over from lunch the day before, but is not enough to cover a full plate of pasta. Pasta is served every day in the Italian fire department.

This is a very hearty dish. An excellent wine to share the meal would be a Barbera, Inferno, or Santa Maddelena.

SERVINGS: 6–8

4 eggs
2½ to 3 cups leftover "gravy" (tomato sauce)
Olive oil
2 pounds fettuccine
1 hot pepper, cut up into small pieces
8 ounces sliced Swiss cheese, chopped
½ cup grated pecorino Romano cheese

Put the water on for the pasta. Meanwhile, beat the eggs and let stand.

In a very large deep skillet heat the leftover gravy. Add just a drop of olive oil to the gravy and stir occasionally over very low heat.

When the water comes to a boil, add the fettuccine and cook until al dente. Drain the pasta, rinse quickly, and add to the skillet with the leftover gravy.

Raise the heat to a medium-to-high flame. Add the hot pepper, eggs, and Swiss cheese. Mix well over the heat until the eggs are no longer watery and the Swiss cheese is melted. If it seems too dry, add some more olive oil. Sprinkle the grated pecorino Romano cheese over the top.

Station Chief Gilberto Driusi
Engine 12-A, Tuscolana II, Fire Department, Rome, Italy

Main Courses
Fish

Swordfish Kabobs/*Hillery*

Cod Fillet, Barbecue Style/*Sineno*

Popeye's Delight, or Pesce Verde/*Daley*

Stuffed Flounder/*DeLusa*

Fillet of Flounder with Shrimp Stuffing/*Catapano*

Seafood Newburg/*Cantley*

Baked Blue-Claw Crabs/*Sineno*

Shrimp Creole à la Faherty/*Faherty*

East Harlem Shrimp/*White*

Broiled Shrimp Scampi/*Stack*

Shrimp in Spicy Sauce/*Ebinger*

Shrimp and Scallops in Wine Sauce/*Ginley*

Shrimp Parmesan/*Sineno*

Shrimp with Sun-Dried Tomatoes and White Clam Sauce

on Pasta/*Sineno*

Scallops Parmesan/*Gerken*

Celtic Mussels/*White*

Tuna Rockefeller/*Thomas*

Out-of-Season Lobster/*Yokley*

Baked Salmon in Foil/*Di Piano and Sineno*

Seafood Casserole/*McLaughlin*

SERVINGS: 6

2½ pounds fresh swordfish
1½ cups vegetable oil
½ cup white vinegar
¼ cup sauterne
1 garlic clove, chopped
1 teaspoon chopped shallots
2 tablespoons chopped fresh dill
1½ teaspoons salt
¼ teaspoon hot pepper sauce
12 pearl onions
12 whole large mushrooms
4 medium green peppers, sliced (¾-inch strips)
12 cherry tomatoes
Hot cooked long-grain white rice
Lemon wedges and parsley sprigs for garnish

Slice the swordfish into 1-inch cubes. In a blender combine the oil, vinegar, sauterne, garlic, shallots, dill, salt, and hot pepper sauce. Blend for 1 minute on high. Pour the marinade over the swordfish in a glass or plastic bowl; cover and refrigerate for 4 to 7 hours.

Cook the pearl onions in boiling water for 8 minutes. Let cool.

Drain the swordfish, reserving the marinade. Arrange the swordfish, pearl onions, mushrooms, and peppers on 6 skewers. Brush with the marinade, then broil or grill 3 to 4 inches from the heat for 7 to 10 minutes. Add the cherry tomatoes (2 per skewer). Baste the kabobs and broil for an additional 2 minutes, or until the tomatoes are tender. Remove the fish and vegetables from the skewers and serve on a bed of rice. Garnish with lemon wedges and parsley sprigs.

NOTE: Although preferably broiled, the kabobs can be baked 15 minutes at 400° F.

Lt. William A. Hillery
Fire Academy, F.D.N.Y.

Cod Fillet, Barbecue Style

SERVINGS: 2

2 medium onions
2 pieces cod fillet (1½ to 2 pounds each)
Salt
Pepper
Paprika
Thinly sliced garlic
Bread crumbs (to coat the fish, as desired)
2 lemons
¼ cup lemon juice
¼ cup water
Chopped fresh parsley

Heat a grill or broiler.

Slice 1 onion and place the slices on a large piece of aluminum foil. Place one cod fillet over the onion. Sprinkle with salt, pepper, paprika, garlic, and bread crumbs to taste. Chop the remaining onion and add, then squeeze one lemon over the toppings. Cover with the second piece of fillet and repeat above process.

Seal the aluminum foil tight, leaving one end open. Pour in a mixture of the lemon juice and water. Seal the foil end and place the package on a grill or broiler rack for 10 to 15 minutes, depending on the thickness of the fish. Garnish with parsley to serve.

John Sineno, retired
Engine 58, F.D.N.Y.

POPEYE'S DELIGHT,
OR PESCE VERDE

Serve with fresh French or Italian bread and white wine.

SERVINGS: 4

1 pound fresh spinach, stemmed and rinsed
2 pounds scrod fillets
1 stick (½ cup) butter or margarine
3 garlic cloves, finely chopped
1 red bell pepper
8 ounces fresh mushrooms
1 medium onion, chopped
1 large tomato, chopped
5 ounces scallops
5 ounces medium shrimp, shelled, deveined, and halved
Juice of 1 lemon
½ cup grated Romano cheese

Preheat the oven to 350° F.

Cover the bottom of a large baking dish with the spinach. Lay the scrod on top of the spinach. Set aside. Melt the butter in a small frying pan and cook the garlic 2 minutes. Add the remaining vegetables, scallops, and shrimp and simmer 5 minutes while stirring in the lemon juice. Pour the entire mixture over the scrod and spinach. Sprinkle with the grated cheese and bake for 25 minutes.

Capt. Dan Daley
F.D.N.Y.

STUFFED FLOUNDER

SERVINGS: 6

1 small onion, diced
2 garlic cloves, diced
3 tablespoons butter
12 ounces small mushrooms, diced
2 tablespoons chopped fresh parsley
Cayenne pepper
Black pepper
8 ounces bay scallops
8 ounces crab sticks or sea legs, diced
Juice of 1 lemon
¾ cup white wine (optional)
6 flounder fillets (about 4 ounces each)

Preheat the oven to 350° F.

Sauté the onion and garlic in the butter in a skillet. Add the mushrooms and parsley and simmer, stirring occasionally, 5 minutes. Add a pinch each of cayenne pepper and black pepper. Stir in the scallops and crab sticks. Simmer, stirring occasionally, 7 minutes. Add the lemon juice. (Wine optional at this point.)

Place 3 flounder fillets in a shallow baking dish and spoon the stuffing over each; top with the remaining fillets. Bake, covered, 15 minutes.

Tom DeLusa
Engine 321, F.D.N.Y.

FILLET OF FLOUNDER WITH SHRIMP STUFFING

SERVINGS: 2

Vegetable oil
1 flounder fillet (about 1 pound), rinsed
½ pound shrimp, shelled and deveined
Seasoned bread crumbs
Paprika
1 large green bell pepper, chopped
1 medium onion, chopped
1 garlic clove, chopped
6 ounces frozen orange juice
3 ounces frozen lemonade
2 shakes Worcestershire sauce
Salt and black pepper to taste

Preheat the oven to 375° F. Spread oil lightly on the bottom of a baking dish.

Lay the flounder fillet out flat. Coat the shrimp with bread crumbs, then place on one end of the fillet and roll up. (If the shrimp are large they may be boiled for 2 minutes then rolled up in the fillet.) Arrange in the oiled baking dish and sprinkle with paprika; bake until the fillet flakes with a touch of a fork, 10 to 15 minutes, depending on the size and thickness of the fillet.

Meanwhile, make the sauce. Heat 2 tablespoons oil in a frying pan. Add the chopped pepper and cook till tender. Add the onion and garlic and cook 3 minutes. Add the orange juice and lemonade, Worcestershire sauce, salt, and black pepper. Heat, but do not allow the mixture to boil.

Pour the sauce over the cooked fillet and serve.

Tony Catapano
Engine 202, F.D.N.Y.

SEAFOOD NEWBURG

SERVINGS: 2

1 cup diced onion
½ stick (¼ cup) butter
8 ounces shrimp, peeled, deveined, and chopped
8 ounces crabmeat
½ teaspoon salt (optional)
¾ teaspoon pepper
Sherry
½ cup all-purpose flour
1 cup sour cream
Swiss cheese, grated

Preheat the oven to 325° F.

Sauté the onion in the butter in a skillet till tender; do not brown. Add the shrimp and cook till pink. Add the crabmeat, salt, and pepper. Pour in sherry to taste. Gradually add the flour, stirring constantly over very low heat. Simmer 5 minutes. Remove from the heat, add the sour cream, and mix thoroughly. Spoon into a casserole dish and top with Swiss cheese to taste. Bake till the cheese melts.

Lt. William Cantley
Engine 16, F.D.N.Y.

BAKED BLUE-CLAW CRABS

SERVINGS: 6

2 dozen blue-claw crabs
4 sticks (1 pound) margarine
1 can (16 ounces) Spanish-style tomato sauce
Garlic powder
Onion powder
Parsley flakes
Dried oregano
½ cup water

Preheat the oven to 400° F.

Take the backs off the crabs and clean. Place in a roasting pan. Melt margarine and drizzle over the crabs. Pour on the tomato sauce. Season with garlic powder, onion powder, parsley, and oregano to taste. Pour the water around the crabs and bake till the crabs are pink in color, 20 to 30 minutes.

John Sineno, retired
Engine 58, F.D.N.Y.

A fireman and his wife told me that their daughter had gotten married and that they had given her the book as a gift. After being married for six months, she invited both families over for diner, whereupon her father told her mother not to forget the Alka-Seltzer because their daughter did not know how to cook and had a history of burning water in the kitchen!

It so happened that the daughter put a terrific three- or four-course meal together that day. Her father couldn't get over it and asked her where she'd learned to cook like that. She replied that it was "the book you gave me, Dad." Her father couldn't believe it, and immediately expressed the desire that I come out with another book soon!

John Sineno

SHRIMP CREOLE À LA FAHERTY

SERVINGS: 2

½ stick (¼ cup) butter
1 large onion, chopped
1 cup minced green bell pepper
1 garlic clove, minced
1 teaspoon salt
Dash of pepper
¼ teaspoon dried rosemary
⅛ teaspoon paprika
2 cups stewed tomatoes
1 pound cooked, shelled, and deveined shrimp
2 to 3 cups hot cooked long-grain white rice

Melt the butter in a large saucepan. Add the onion, green pepper, and garlic and sauté 10 minutes. Add the salt, pepper, rosemary, paprika, and tomatoes and bring to a boil. Reduce the heat and simmer for about 15 minutes. Add the shrimp and heat thoroughly.

Serve on a bed of fluffy hot rice.

Lt. T. Faherty
Brooklyn/Queens Holy Name Society

Have everything prepared and ready to go.

SERVINGS: 4

Chow Sauce
1 tablespoon Worcestershire sauce
1 tablespoon dry sherry
2 tablespoons ketchup
¼ cup water
2 tablespoons sugar
½ teaspoon salt
1½ teaspoons cornstarch

Shrimp
1 teaspoon salt
1 pound large shrimp, shelled and deveined
2½ tablespoons vegetable oil
4 large garlic cloves, minced
1 heaping teaspoon minced fresh ginger
½ teaspoon crushed red pepper
5 or 6 green onions, green part and all, thinly sliced

Mix the ingredients for the chow sauce in a small bowl and set aside.

Rub the salt into the shrimp. Let it stand for about 15 minutes, then rinse well and dry with paper towels.

Heat 1½ tablespoons of oil in a wide pan or wok over medium heat. Add the shrimp and stir-fry until they turn pink. Remove the shrimp and set aside. Heat the rest of the oil and stir-fry the garlic, ginger, and red pepper for just a few seconds. Return the shrimp to the pan along with the green onions. Stir in the chow sauce, and keep stirring until the sauce becomes thick.

Bill White
Ladder 164, F.D.N.Y.

BROILED SHRIMP SCAMPI

SERVINGS: 3–4

1½ to 2 pounds jumbo or large shrimp, shelled and deveined
1½ sticks (¾ cup) butter or margarine, melted
½ cup chopped fresh parsley
6 garlic cloves, crushed
2 teaspoons lemon juice
½ teaspoon salt
¼ teaspoon pepper
¾ cup vegetable oil

Heat the broiler.

Place the shrimp on a broiler pan. Combine all the other ingredients and pour over the shrimp. Broil 4 inches from the heat for 4 minutes. Turn the shrimp and broil for 3 more minutes. Serve.

NOTE: Some chefs use the broiler pan without the top grill—this allows the shrimp to absorb more of the sauce.

Tom Stack
Brooklyn/Queens Holy Name Society

SERVINGS: 12–15

2 pounds medium shrimp
1 small shallot, chopped
1 cup chopped or sliced onion
1 tablespoon crushed garlic
2 small jalapeño peppers, chopped
1 cup peeled, seeded, and diced tomatoes
1 tablespoon turmeric
1 tablespoon ground cumin
1 tablespoon crushed red pepper
1 teaspoon ground nutmeg
1½ teaspoons pepper
¼ cup heavy cream
8 ounces plain yogurt
2 tablespoons poppy seeds

Peel and devein the shrimp; set aside. Make a stock by simmering the shrimp shells in 2 cups water for 30 minutes. Strain and reserve 1 cup of the stock.

In a large saucepan, sweat the shallot, onion, and garlic, covered, until translucent. Add the shrimp, jalapeños, tomatoes, and all spices (except the poppy seeds). Stir and simmer about 10 minutes.

Add the shrimp stock and cream and simmer until the liquid reduces by half. Add the yogurt and let thicken by reduction; do not allow to boil.

In a dry skillet, toss the poppy seeds on medium to low heat, shaking the pan to prevent burning. Crush the seeds with the back of a spoon or in a mortar when done. Add the roasted poppy seeds before serving.

Paul M. Ebinger
Governors Island Firehouse

SHRIMP AND SCALLOPS IN WINE SAUCE

SERVINGS: 12

3 pounds medium shrimp, shelled and deveined
3 pounds bay scallops
½ cup vegetable oil
½ stick (¼ cup) butter
½ cup cornstarch
4 to 6 cups milk (depending upon desired consistency)
1½ cups white wine
6 cups hot cooked long-grain white rice

Sauté the shrimp and scallops lightly in the oil until just done. Set aside. Slowly melt butter in a large pot. Add the cornstarch, then the milk, stirring constantly until thickened. Add the wine, shrimp, and scallops.

Serve over hot cooked rice.

Joe Ginley, retired
Engine 8, F.D.N.Y.

SHRIMP PARMESAN

SERVINGS: 10

5 pounds large shrimp, shelled and deveined
3 sticks (¾ pound) margarine
8 ounces mozzarella, grated
1 tablespoon garlic powder
1 tablespoon onion powder
5 ounces Parmesan cheese, grated
1 jar (16 ounces) marinara sauce

Preheat the oven to 400° F.

Place the shrimp in a large baking dish. Melt the margarine and pour over the shrimp. Spread evenly with the mozzarella. Sprinkle with the garlic and onion powder and grated Parmesan. Cover with marinara sauce and bake for 15 to 20 minutes.

John Sineno, retired
Engine 58, F.D.N.Y.

SHRIMP WITH SUN-DRIED TOMATOES AND WHITE CLAM SAUCE ON PASTA

SERVINGS: 4–6

8 ounces sun-dried tomatoes, packed in oil
2 pounds medium shrimp
1 cup dry white wine
1 can (15 ounces) white clam sauce
1 can (6½ ounces) minced or chopped clams, drained

Drain the oil from the sun-dried tomatoes into a deep frying pan and sauté the shrimp in it until the shrimp are pink in color. Chop and toss the sun-dried tomatoes. Add the white wine and let the mixture come to a boil, then turn off the flame. Prepare the pasta of your choice (linguine, spaghetti, etcetera). Turn the flame on again and add the can of white clam sauce. Once that has simmered for a bit, add the drained chopped or minced clams on a high flame. Once the mixture has boiled, turn off the flame.

This is an easy dish to make and very delicious.

Enjoy!

John Sineno, retired
Engine 58, F.D.N.Y.

Christmas Eve Dinner

Fireman Joe Regan
Engine 73, Ladder 42, Battalion 55, F.D.N.Y.

During my probie year, my turn to work came up, and it was Christmas Eve. Hey, I can't let this be a lost opportunity, I thought. Word got around the firehouse that "Regan is bringing in the meal." I entered the firehouse with all the raw materials for a wonderful meal. Soon the kitchen began to take on the air of a festive occasion, and before long all the members from both houses were chopping, mixing, singing, and joking. When the men discovered that I had brought in candelabras, they took it upon themselves to meticulously set the table, complete with bedsheets as tablecloths.

What a spread it was: flounder in a special white sauce with shallots, breaded and fried shrimp, good hard loaves of crusty semolina, and, of course, mountains of pasta topped with deliciously deep, dark, inky-red calamari. To make the night even more special, we didn't have one run during the preparation and eating. In our busy neighborhood, this was a rare and welcome treat.

The next day, Christmas, several firehouses from the neighborhood joined us at our quarters to celebrate Christmas in a religious service. The priest did his best to prepare a respectable altar, but sadly lamented that "If only we had some nice candles, what a beautiful touch that would bring!" Well, say no more—yesterday's table setting became today's altar—bedsheets and candelabras and all. Oh, that meal went a long, long way.

The volunteer fire service attracts men and women from all walks of life.

This was illustrated one evening at the Bethpage training center when I walked into a conversation with two fellow officers from

the Plandome Volunteer Department, with whom my company from the Bellerose Village F.D. was working that evening. One chief remarked that he used a vehicle that had over 1,000,000 miles on its odometer. I couldn't imagine a volunteer department ever running that many miles on any piece of apparatus. When I asked some questions, I found out that the apparatus was a tour bus that was used by the Guy Lombardo Orchestra, and the name of that Plandome chief was Ken Lane, the orchestra's lead singer for many years.

SCALLOPS PARMESAN

SERVINGS: 3–4, DEPENDING ON APPETITE

2 pounds scallops (Long Island Peconic Bay scallops if available)
3 garlic cloves, chopped
1 green onion, green part and all, chopped
2 tablespoons olive oil
¼ cup grated Parmesan cheese
¼ cup seasoned bread crumbs
Juice of 1 lemon
Salt and white pepper to taste

Preheat oven to 350° F.

If using ocean scallops, cut into smaller pieces. Rinse the scallops and pat dry.

Sauté the chopped garlic and green onion in the olive oil until the garlic and onions soften. Pour the sautéed mixture over the scallops on a nonstick cookie sheet and bake for 9 to 10 minutes. Sprinkle a mixture of the Parmesan cheese and bread crumbs over the scallops and broil for 2 to 3 minutes, until the scallops brown slightly. Turn if necessary.

Sprinkle the lemon juice over the scallops and add salt and white pepper to taste before eating.

Former Chief Fred Gerken
Bellerose Village Fire Department, Bellerose, New York

CELTIC MUSSELS

As you no doubt know, St. Patrick invented pasta. It was later brought to Italy by Marco Polo.

SERVINGS: 2–4

8 ounces spinach linguine
8 ounces regular linguine
½ stick (¼ cup) butter
1 tablespoon vegetable oil
1 each green and red bell pepper, finely diced
4 or 5 garlic cloves, chopped
2 to 3 pounds mussels, scrubbed and debearded
1 cup dry white wine
1 cup bottled clam juice
1 tablespoon cornstarch
1 good healthy pinch (or about ¼ teaspoon) saffron

Prepare the pasta according to package directions.

Meanwhile, melt the butter and the oil in a big enough saucepan to hold all the mussels. Sauté the peppers and garlic until soft. Add the mussels and wine all at once. Raise the heat to medium high, cover the pot, and agitate on the heat until the mussels open and give up their juices. Remove the mussels.

To the liquid remaining in the pan add the clam juice, in which the cornstarch has been dissolved, and the saffron. Simmer until the liquid becomes clear.

Dump the mussels on a bed of prepared pasta and pour the sauce over all. If you like, you can have just the mussels and sauce in a bowl and skip the pasta.

Bill White
Ladder 164, F.D.N.Y.

Serve with rice pilaf or brown rice and a tomato-onion salad.

SERVINGS: 4 (OR ENOUGH FOR 2 FIREMEN)

1 pound fresh spinach
8 ounces bacon
½ cup seasoned bread crumbs
4 ounces Parmesan cheese, grated
1 container (8 ounces) sour cream
Salt and pepper to taste
1 medium-size lemon
2 cans (7 ounces each) white-meat tuna

Preheat the oven to 350° F.

Rinse the spinach carefully in a pot of clear water. Do it a second time. Cook the spinach in a covered saucepan containing a small amount of water over medium-high heat. In just a few moments, when the spinach is soft, drain it and chop it as fine as you can. You may want to run it through a blender.

Fry the bacon in a large frying pan over medium heat, turning the bacon once and then draining it on paper towels.

Put the chopped spinach into a baking dish and add the bacon, crumbled into pieces. Then add the seasoned bread crumbs, about half the grated Parmesan cheese, half the sour cream, some salt and pepper, and juice of half the lemon. Finally, open the cans of tuna, drain away the liquid, and flake the tuna over the mixture. Add the remaining sour cream and lemon juice. Sprinkle the rest of the Parmesan cheese over the top. Put the baking dish into the oven. It will be ready in 20 minutes.

Bill Thomas
President, Emerald Society
Aide to Chief of Department, F.D.N.Y.

OUT-OF-SEASON LOBSTER

As a scuba diver, one enjoys a good lobster as often as possible. However, I've discovered I don't have to suffer (too much) when the feisty critters are out of season. This recipe holds me over until the season opens again.

SERVINGS: 6

2 pounds white fish fillets
1 bay leaf
1 small onion, sliced
3 lemon slices
½ cup dry (white) vermouth
Melted butter
Parsley and lemon wedges for garnish

Place the fish in a deep saucepan. Cover with water. Add the bay leaf, onion, lemon slices, and vermouth. Bring to a boil, then reduce to a simmer for 8 to 10 minutes, or until the fish starts to break apart.

Remove from the pan. Serve with melted butter and garnished with lemon wedges and parsley.

Capt. Richard Yokley
Engine 12, Bonita Fire Department, Bonita, California

BAKED SALMON IN FOIL

SERVINGS: 4

4 pieces (3½ ounces each) of salmon
8 fresh mushrooms, sliced
1 onion, cut into rings
1 large carrot, peeled and cut into sticks
4 lemon wedges
¼ cup sherry or white wine

Preheat the oven to 350° F.

Cut 4 sheets of foil. On each foil sheet put a piece of salmon, some mushrooms, onion rings, carrots, and a lemon wedge. Sprinkle with the sherry or wine. Seal each packet tight, put on a baking sheet, and bake for 12 to 15 minutes.

NOTE: You can serve this with rice. Bring 1 cup of rice and 2½ cups water to a boil on a high heat. Lower to a simmer with the cover on and cook 12 to 14 minutes. You can add some saffron for color or taste; you can also add some fresh steamed veggies to the rice dish.

Pete Di Piano
Engine 325, F.D.N.Y.
John Sineno, retired
Engine 58, F.D.N.Y.

SEAFOOD CASSEROLE

Serve this with a garden salad.

SERVINGS: 10

2 pounds haddock, cod, or any white fish fillets
2½ pounds large shrimp, shelled and deveined
2 pounds sea scallops
2 pounds imitation crabmeat
1 pint heavy cream, plus milk if necessary
½ cup parsley flakes
1 small onion, chopped
2 stalks celery, chopped
2 shallots, chopped
1 stick (½ cup) butter
Enough bread crumbs to cover

Preheat the oven to 325° F.

Cut up the fish and place in 13 x 9 x 2-inch baking dish. Add the shrimp, scallops, and crabmeat. Pour the cream over the ingredients and add milk to cover if necessary. Add the parsley flakes.

In a frying pan sauté the chopped onion, celery, and shallots in the butter till they wilt and the onions are clear. Toss this with the other ingredients and cover with a light coating of bread crumbs. Bake for approximately 30 minutes, or until the cream starts to bubble up.

Lt. Austin F. McLaughlin
Rescue Co. 2, Dis. II, Boston, Massachusetts

Main Courses
Poultry

Quick Chicken and Rice/*Sineno*

Norma's Amazing Chicken/*O'Donnell*

Stuffed Chicken over Rice/*Di Piano and Sineno*

Hawaiian Chicken/*Auletta*

Elegant Orange Chicken/*Finn*

Chicken Marsala/*Sherwood*

Chicken or Veal in Wine Sauce/*Munday*

Chicken Fontina with Portobello Mushrooms/*Gambino*

Oriental Chicken/*Kessler*

Seasoned Fried Chicken/*Donnelly*

Low Tide Chicken/*Hill*

Chicken with Walnuts/*Scheu*

Chicken Adobo/*Fields*

New Orleans Jambalaya/*Shea*

Italian-Style Chicken/*Genovese*

Chicken Breasts with Accidental Sauce/*Sineno*

Barbecued Chicken/*Sineno*

Chicken/Vegetable Medley/*LoFaso*

Chicken Lasagne/*Anderson*

Chicken Enchiladas/*Neider*

Turkey Curry "à la Gin"/*Ginley*

Turkey au Gratin/*Loper*

Best Batch Turkey Chili/*Newman*

Deputy Chief Joyce's Italian Turkey Meatloaf/*Joyce*

QUICK CHICKEN AND RICE

SERVINGS: 6

2 tablespoons vegetable oil
1 chicken (3 pounds), cut into 8 pieces
1 onion, diced
1 garlic clove, minced
1 large can tomato sauce
Dried basil
Dried oregano
Salt and pepper
2 cups long-grain white rice
4 cups water

Heat the oil in a Dutch oven and brown the chicken, onion, and garlic. Add the tomato sauce and basil, oregano, salt, and pepper to taste. Cook till chicken is tender.

In a separate pot, cook the rice in the water according to package directions. Pour the chicken and sauce over the rice to serve.

John Sineno, retired
Engine 58, F.D.N.Y.

NORMA'S AMAZING CHICKEN

This is good with cucumber and yogurt salad.

SERVINGS: 4–6

1 tablespoon ground allspice
1 tablespoon salt
1 tablespoon pepper
¾ cup vegetable oil
1 head cauliflower, cut up
1 cup long-grain white rice
1 16-ounce can chicken broth
3 large onions, diced
1 chicken (2 to 3½ pounds), cut up

Preheat the oven to 350° F. Mix the allspice, salt, and pepper.

Heat ¼ cup oil in a large skillet over medium heat. Add the cauliflower and 1 tablespoon of the seasoning mix and cook, stirring, until browned. Pour over the rice and chicken broth in a baking pan. Repeat with the onions and chicken, using the rest of the oil and seasoning mix, and layer on the rice. Cover with foil and bake for 1 hour.

Capt. Jim O'Donnell

SERVINGS: 4

1 onion, chopped
3 tablespoons butter, melted
¼ cup chopped fresh parsley
½ cup chopped fresh mushrooms
Pinch of black pepper
1 cup seasoned bread crumbs
1 pound chicken cutlets, thinly sliced
1 or 2 cans cream of mushroom soup
1 cup rice
2½ cups water

Preheat the oven to 350° F.

In a bowl combine the onion, butter, parsley, mushrooms, pepper, and bread crumbs and make a stuffing mix.

Put some of the stuffing on each cutlet and roll it. Tie or use toothpicks to hold the rolls together. Brown lightly in butter in a frying pan on all sides. Put in a baking dish, cover with cream of mushroom soup, and bake for 30 minutes.

Meanwhile, bring the rice and water to a boil in a saucepan on high heat. Lower heat to a simmer with the cover on and cook 12 to 14 minutes.

Serve the chicken over the rice.

Pete Di Piano,
Engine 325, F.D.N.Y.
John Sineno, retired
Engine 58, F.D.N.Y.

Hawaiian Chicken

SERVINGS: 4

2 pounds skinless, boneless chicken breasts
½ cup all-purpose flour
6 tablespoons vegetable oil
2 tablespoons butter
4 garlic cloves, finely chopped
1 large or 2 small onions, cut into ½-inch strips
3 green bell peppers, cut into 1-inch chunks
½ cup (packed) brown sugar
⅓ cup white vinegar
1 can (15 ounces) pineapple chunks
2 medium tomatoes, cut into eighths
Salt and pepper
Gravy Master
Hot cooked long-grain white rice (optional)

Clean and trim the fat from the chicken breasts. Cut in half lengthwise, creating 2 separate breasts. Cut the breasts into pieces about 1½ inches square. Coat the pieces thoroughly with flour and brown in 3 tablespoons of the oil in a frying pan over medium heat until the pieces are golden. Drain on paper towels and set aside.

In a 5-quart saucepan, heat the remaining oil and the butter over medium heat and sauté the garlic, onion, and peppers until thoroughly mixed and coated with oil. In a separate bowl combine the brown sugar and vinegar. Mix and add to the garlic, onion, and pepper mixture. Add the undrained pineapple chunks and chicken pieces to the vegetable mixture and stir. Simmer, covered, over low heat about 25 minutes, stirring occasionally.

Stir in the tomatoes and salt and pepper to taste. Cover and let simmer another 5 minutes. If necessary, add flour to thicken. Stir in Gravy Master to darken the mixture to the desired color. Cover, remove from the heat, and let stand for 5 minutes.

Serve either separately or over rice.

Paul E. Auletta
Ladder 103, F.D.N.Y.

If there are any hunters in the firehouse, this recipe goes well with pheasant, grouse, duck, and woodcock.

SERVINGS: 6

¾ stick (⅓ cup) butter
¼ cup all-purpose flour
¾ teaspoon ground cinnamon
1½ cups orange juice
6 tablespoons orange marmalade
2 teaspoons instant chicken bouillon
6 skinless, boneless chicken breast halves
2 cups green seedless grapes
2 cups mandarin orange slices
Hot cooked long-grain white rice
¾ cup sliced almonds, roasted
Baked Carrots (recipe below)

Preheat the oven to 350° F.

Melt the butter in a saucepan. Sir in the flour and cinnamon until smooth. Blend in the orange juice, marmalade, and bouillon, bring to a boil, and stir until thickened. Place the chicken in a single layer in a large square baking dish. Pour the above mixture over the chicken, seal with foil, and bake for 45 minutes, or until the chicken is cooked.

Add the grapes and orange slices to the top of the chicken and bake, uncovered, 5 to 10 minutes longer, or until the fruit is heated.

Serve over rice, sprinkled with the almonds; serve accompanied by the carrots.

BAKED CARROTS

SERVINGS: 6

2 pounds carrots
1 stick (½ cup) butter

Wash the carrots but do not peel. Cut in half lengthwise, or about 3 inches long. Cut these into quarters to make carrot sticks. Place in a deep baking dish, put the butter on top, and bake, covered, for 45 minutes, or the full time for the above chicken recipe.

Tom Finn
Ladder Co. 2, Boston Fire Department, Boston, Massachusetts

CHICKEN MARSALA

Serve this with noodles Alfredo.

SERVINGS: 4

2 sticks (1 cup) butter
¼ cup olive oil
2 pounds chicken cutlets, pounded and cut into medallion-size pieces
All-purpose flour
Salt and pepper to taste
1 pound fresh mushrooms
1 shallot
1½ cups sweet Marsala wine
1 bunch parsley, minced
2 lemons, halved

Preheat the oven to 350° F.

Melt one stick of the butter in a skillet and add the olive oil. Dredge the chicken in flour seasoned with salt and pepper. Shake off excess and sauté in the butter and oil to golden brown. Place the chicken in an ovenproof pan and set aside.

Separate the mushroom caps from stems. Mince the mushroom stems with the shallot and quarter or slice the mushroom caps. Melt the remaining 1 stick of butter in the skillet and sauté the shallots and mushrooms, cooking until the mushrooms release their juice. Remove from the heat and add the wine and 1 tablespoon of the minced parsley. Season to taste and simmer for 5 minutes.

While the mixture is simmering, squeeze the juice of the 2 lemons over the chicken. Pour the sauce mixture over the chicken, cover, and bake for 15 to 20 minutes. Garnish with the remaining parsley.

Jim Sherwood
Ladder 19, F.D.N.Y.

The probie, or rookie, usually gets to go to the store to purchase the ingredients for the company's meals. It's the same in all jobs— the low man on the totem pole gets to do everything everyone else wants to avoid. Anyway, one afternoon I sent a probie to the store with a list of things I needed for the meal. One was a bottle of white wine to be used to baste the roast chicken.

When the probie returned from the store with his arms full of groceries, I noted that he'd bought red wine instead of white.

"What the hell, I'll use the red," I said.

When I removed the chicken from the oven and set it on the table, all the guys did a double take. The roast chicken was *purple*. It got a good laugh, but I noticed that the color of the chicken didn't diminish anyone's appetite.

From then on I'd occasionally hear someone call out to me as I reported to work, "Hey, Mama, how about making purple chicken tonight?"

John Sineno

CHICKEN OR VEAL IN WINE SAUCE

SERVINGS: 8

4 pounds chicken or veal cutlets, cut in pieces
¾ cup all-purpose flour
1 teaspoon salt
1 teaspoon pepper
1 stick (½ cup) plus 3 tablespoons butter or margarine
1 cup Madeira wine
1 chicken bouillon cube, dissolved in ½ cup water
½ teaspoon chopped garlic
1 pound fresh mushrooms, sliced
1 tablespoon lemon juice

Preheat the oven to 350° F.

Dip the meat in flour seasoned with the salt and pepper. Melt the 1 stick butter and brown the meat in a skillet, in batches, 2 to 3 minutes on each side. Arrange in a large baking dish.

Drain the fat from the skillet. Add the wine, bouillon, and garlic and bring to a boil over medium heat, stirring. Pour over the meat.

Brown the mushrooms in the 3 tablespoons butter in the skillet and sprinkle with the lemon juice. Cover the meat with the mushrooms, then cover the dish with aluminum foil. Bake for 40 to 50 minutes.

Jim Munday
Ladder 156, F.D.N.Y.

CHICKEN FONTINA WITH PORTOBELLO MUSHROOMS

SERVINGS: 6

1 cup all-purpose flour
¼ cup chopped fresh parsley
Salt and pepper to taste
Olive oil
Margarine
1½ pounds chicken cutlets, pounded thin
1 bunch young asparagus spears
1 can (8 ounces) beef broth
⅓ cup Marsala wine
2 large portobello mushrooms, sliced
4 ounces thinly sliced prosciutto
8 ounces thinly sliced Italian Fontina cheese

Preheat the oven to 350° F. Thoroughly mix the flour, parsley, salt, and pepper.

Heat a large frying pan and add oil and margarine, as needed to fry. Lightly flour the chicken in the parsley mixture and fry, in batches, in the hot frying pan 2 to 3 minutes on each side. Remove to a baking dish.

Meanwhile, steam the asparagus till tender, 10 to 15 minutes.

Remove excess grease from the frying pan (don't wash). Add the beef broth, wine, mushrooms, salt, and pepper. Bring to a boil and deglaze the pan. Lower the heat and simmer 10 minutes.

Place the slices of prosciutto on the chicken. Top each cutlet with slices of cheese. Then place 1 asparagus spear on each cutlet. Place in the oven and bake 15 to 20 minutes, until the cheese melts. Serve accompanied by the mushrooms.

Frank Gambino
Ladder 26, F.D.N.Y.

Serve with this rice, snow peas, and Chinese noodles.

SERVINGS: 8

½ cup sesame oil
½ cup soy sauce
¼ cup minced fresh ginger
2 pounds chicken cutlets
Vegetable oil
1 cup chicken broth
1 stick (½ cup) butter, melted
4 teaspoons dry mustard (made into a paste with a small amount of water)

Mix the sesame oil, soy sauce, and 2 teaspoons of the ginger. Marinate the chicken for at least 1 hour, but no longer than 2 days. In a skillet fry 1 minute on each side in small amount of vegetable oil. Drain on paper towels. Wipe out the skillet.

In the skillet combine the chicken broth, butter, remaining ginger, and the mustard paste. Add chicken to the pan and cover. Cook slowly for 30 minutes, or until done. Place the chicken on a platter and cover with the sauce.

Warren G. Kessler, retired
Engine 268, F.D.N.Y.

SERVINGS: 4

3 skinless, boneless chicken breast halves (about 3 pounds)
½ cup soy sauce
1 tablespoon grated fresh ginger
1 tablespoon lemon juice
2 tablespoons sake or dry sherry
1½ cups coarse bread crumbs, purchased or homemade
⅓ cup all-purpose flour
2 tablespoons cornstarch
2 eggs
Peanut oil

Cut the chicken into 1-inch square chunks. In a bowl combine the soy sauce, ginger, lemon juice, and sake. Reserve a small portion of marinade before it touches the raw meat, then stir the chicken into the remainder. Cover and let stand at room temperature for about 30 minutes, stirring occasionally. Drain the chicken and pat dry.

Place the bread crumbs in a pie pan. In a second pie pan, combine the flour and cornstarch. In a third pie pan, lightly beat the eggs. Dredge the chicken pieces in flour mixture; shake off excess. Dip in the egg, then roll in the crumbs.

Meanwhile, pour peanut oil into a 2½-to-3-quart saucepan to a depth of 2 inches and heat to 375° F on a deep-frying thermometer. Fry the chicken, a few pieces at a time, until the coating is browned on all sides and the meat is no longer pink in the center when slashed (about 2 minutes). Drain briefly on paper towels and serve immediately. Use the reserved marinade as a dipping sauce.

John Donnelly
Ladder 125, F.D.N.Y.

LOW TIDE CHICKEN

This will look like low tide on the beach if done correctly.

SERVINGS: 12

½ cup olive oil
1 teaspoon chopped garlic clove
All-purpose flour
6 pounds chicken cutlets
1½ cups water
4 chicken bouillon cubes
1 teaspoon dried thyme
¼ teaspoon salt
Pepper
1 pound fresh mushrooms, sliced
5 packages (10 ounces each) frozen leaf spinach
Hot cooked long-grain white rice

Preheat the oven to 350° F.

Heat the olive oil in a large skillet and sauté the garlic. Flour the chicken and fry lightly on both sides in the garlic oil, then place in a roasting pan. Strain the oil, saving approximately ¼ cup. Pour the oil back into the skillet and add the water, bouillon cubes, thyme, salt, and pepper. Cook on high heat until the water has almost boiled away, then add the mushrooms. Sauté over a low flame for 10 minutes.

In a large saucepan, cook the spinach as per directions on the package. Drain and spread over the chicken. Pour the mushrooms and sauce over the spinach. Bake for 10 minutes and serve over rice.

Howard Hill
Ladder 9, F.D.N.Y.

Serves great with rice.

SERVINGS: 6–8 (OR 3 FIREMEN)

2 to 3 pounds chicken breasts, split, or 2 chicken cutlets or chicken breasts per
   person
1 egg
½ cup milk
½ cup all-purpose flour
1 tablespoon baking powder
1 tablespoon sea salt
½ teaspoon cayenne pepper
⅛ teaspoon black pepper
1 teaspoon paprika
½ cup walnuts
1 stick (½ cup) butter

Preheat the oven to 350° F.

Skin and remove the fat on the chicken (optional). Beat the egg and milk in
a bowl. Put the flour, baking powder, salt, spices, and walnuts in a paper bag
after you have either combined everything in a blender or pounded it with a
mallet.

Dip the chicken in the egg mixture. Shake in the bag until coated well, then
put in a baking pan or dish. Melt the butter and pour over the chicken. Bake
for 35 to 40 minutes.

J. Barry Scheu
Garden City Fire Department, Garden City, New York

CHICKEN ADOBO

Don't let the vinegar here mislead you. This is what makes it taste so good. It smells strong at first, but after it simmers awhile, the strong smell of vinegar lessens. You may find that you like more soy sauce. Just add it in until it suits you. The same with the other ingredients. More or less of anything (to your taste) won't hurt a thing. You can add other things as well, celery, string beans, peas, etc. You can serve it on a bed of rice or just add the rice right in. Noodles are good, too. You can also add a can of Chinese vegetables. If you have everything ready, you can make the whole thing in about 20 minutes.

SERVINGS: 4

2 tablespoons vegetable oil
1½ pounds chicken, cut up
1 large onion, chopped
2 garlic cloves, chopped
Pepper
2 tablespoons soy sauce
2 tablespoons vinegar
Paprika

Heat the oil in a large skillet. Add cut-up chicken. (You can use pork also. Pork and chicken together is very good. You can cut up a whole chicken with a large hammer and a knife, or you can just use chicken breasts cut up, or just white-meat fillets.) While the chicken is cooking, add the chopped onion, garlic, and pepper. Next add the soy sauce and the vinegar and paprika to taste. Simmer, covered, until done.

Walter Fields
Boston Engine 5, East Boston, Massachusetts

SERVINGS: 8–10

2 to 3 pounds chicken, cut up
½ cup olive or vegetable oil
3 cups diced cooked ham
2 garlic cloves, minced
3 small onions, chopped
3 cans (16 ounces each) peeled whole tomatoes
2 teaspoons salt
¼ to ½ teaspoon hot pepper sauce
1 large bay leaf
3 cups diced celery
1 pound shrimp, shelled and deveined
2 cups long-grain white rice
½ cup chopped parsley

In a 5-quart kettle, brown the chicken in the oil. Take the chicken out and set it aside. Brown the ham in the oil, then stir in the garlic and onions and sauté for 5 minutes. Return the chicken to the kettle. Stir in the tomatoes, salt, hot pepper sauce, and bay leaf. Bring to a boil, then reduce the heat, cover, and simmer for 30 minutes.

Stir in the celery, shrimp, and white rice, making sure all the rice is covered by liquid. Simmer 30 minutes longer, or until the chicken and rice are tender. Remove the bay leaf and add the parsley.

Lt. J. Shea
Brooklyn/Queens Holy Name Society

ITALIAN-STYLE CHICKEN

SERVINGS: 4

1 egg
⅔ cup sour cream
1 cup bread crumbs
¼ cup grated pecorino Romano cheese
2½ pounds chicken, cut up

Preheat the oven to 350° F.

Mix the egg with the sour cream in a pie dish. Mix the bread crumbs and pecorino cheese in another dish. Dip chicken parts into the egg and sour cream mixture, then roll in the bread crumbs. Bake in a lightly oiled baking dish for 40 to 50 minutes.

Dominic A. Genovese
Engine 224, F.D.N.Y.

CHICKEN BREASTS WITH ACCIDENTAL SAUCE

Serve this over rice or noodles.

SERVINGS: 6–8

2 pounds skinless, boneless chicken breasts
¼ cup vegetable oil
2 garlic cloves, sliced
Accidental Sauce (see page 50)
½ cup grated Locatelli cheese

Preheat the oven to 375° F.

Slice the chicken into 1-inch-thick cutlets. Heat the oil in a large skillet on a medium-high flame. Add the garlic and fry till golden brown, then add the chicken. Brown on each side and remove to a baking dish.

Prepare the Accidental Sauce and pour over the chicken, then top with the cheese and bake for 30 to 35 minutes, till bubbly.

John Sineno, retired
Engine 58, F.D.N.Y.

BARBECUED CHICKEN

SERVINGS: 12–16

4 whole chickens, quartered
3 cups water
Garlic powder
Onion powder
Paprika
Black pepper
Sugar
1 bottle (44 ounces) ketchup
⅓ cup A.1 sauce
¼ cup Worcestershire sauce
¼ cup lemon juice

Preheat the oven to 400° F.

Place the chicken in a large roasting pan. Add 2 cups of the water. Roast in the oven for about ½ hour. Remove from the oven and drain the juices from the pan; leave the oven on. Sprinkle the chicken to taste with garlic and onion powder, paprika, and black pepper. Take a handful of sugar and sprinkle generously over the chicken.

In a large bowl stir the ketchup, A.1 sauce, Worcestershire sauce, and lemon juice to mix well. Pour the mixture over the chicken. Pour the remaining 1 cup water around the chicken. Return to the oven till the top of the chicken is crisp, about ½ hour. Remove to a platter and serve.

John Sineno, retired
Engine 58, F.D.N.Y.

CHICKEN/VEGETABLE MEDLEY

SERVINGS: 8

6 packages (13 ounces each) cheese tortellini
4 pounds chicken cutlets, cubed
2 tablespoons adobo seasoning
2 cups olive oil
2 small onions, diced
4 medium garlic cloves, diced fine
6 zucchini, chopped
2 cans (13 ounces each) chicken broth
1 cup cold water
3 heaping tablespoons all-purpose flour
2 heads broccoli, cut up and parboiled
3 tablespoons chopped fresh parsley
3 tablespoons chopped fresh basil
6 medium plum tomatoes, diced chunky

Cook the tortellini according to package directions. Marinate the chicken in the adobo seasoning.

In a large wok or skillet, heat the oil to 350° F on a deep-frying thermometer. Add the chicken and blanch, stirring often. When the chicken is ready, remove the excess oil and move the chicken to the sides of the wok and add the onion and garlic. Sauté until glazed. Mix in the chicken. Add the chopped zucchini and stir 4 to 5 minutes until the zucchini is glazed. Add the chicken broth. Simmer 5 minutes.

While simmering, mix the water into the flour and let stand. Add the broccoli, parsley, and basil to the wok. Add the tomatoes, pour in the flour-and-water mixture, and mix until the desired thickness is reached.

When the tortellini are ready, drain and put into dishes. Spoon the chicken mixture over the tortellini.

Jim LoFaso
Engine 283, F.D.N.Y.

CHICKEN LASAGNE

SERVINGS: 6–8

1 whole chicken (3½ to 4 pounds)
9 lasagne noodles
½ stick (¼ cup) margarine or butter
8 ounces fresh mushrooms
2 garlic cloves, chopped
½ teaspoon salt
1 tablespoon lemon juice
¼ cup flour
2 teaspoons chicken bouillon
3 cups milk
½ cup chopped fresh parsley
1 container (15 ounces) ricotta cheese
8 ounces mozzarella cheese, shredded
½ cup grated Parmesan cheese

Prepare the lasagne noodles according to package directions. Boil the chicken in water in a second pot until the meat is fully cooked.

Preheat the oven to 325° F.

In a large saucepan, melt the margarine or butter. Add the mushrooms, garlic, salt, and lemon juice. Sauté until the mushrooms are tender, about 5 minutes.

Stir in the flour and chicken bouillon; blend well. Add the milk. Cook over medium-high heat until the mixture thickens and boils, stirring constantly. Remove from the heat and prepare the chicken.

Skin the chicken, remove it from the bones, and cut the meat into 1½-inch pieces. Mix chicken and ⅓ cup of the parsley into the sauce.

Spread ½ cup of the sauce in the bottom of a 13 x 9 x 2-inch baking pan. Layer one third each of the noodles, ricotta cheese, mozzarella cheese, and sauce. Repeat with two more layers, ending with Parmesan cheese. Sprinkle with the remaining parsley.

Bake for 45 minutes. Let stand for 10 to 15 minutes before serving.

Tom Anderson
Engine Co. 9, Madison, Wisconsin

CHICKEN ENCHILADAS

SERVINGS: 8–10

4 to 5 pounds skinless, boneless chicken breasts, cut into chunks
¼ cup crushed red pepper
⅛ cup chili powder
¼ cup cayenne pepper
⅛ cup Cajun seasoning
2 tablespoons garlic salt
Salt to taste
4 cans (12 ounces each) enchilada sauce
3 packages flour tortillas
1½ pounds cheddar cheese, shredded

Preheat the oven to 350° F.

Brown the chicken in a nonstick skillet with the seasonings. Spread a large baking pan with some of the enchilada sauce. Fill a tortilla with 2 tablespoons chicken and add some cheese. Roll up and place in the pan. Repeat with the remaining tortillas, setting remaining chicken and cheese aside. Pour the remaining sauce over the tortillas. Place the remaining chicken over the sauce, then sprinkle with the cheese. Bake for 30 minutes.

Sondra Neider
Firefighter, U.S. Coast Guard

SERVINGS: 12

½ cup finely chopped onion
½ cup finely chopped celery
½ stick (¼ cup) margarine
⅓ cup cornstarch
2 cups chicken stock or broth
1 cup tomato juice
½ teaspoon Worcestershire sauce
1 teaspoon curry powder
Pepper to taste
5 pounds diced cooked turkey breast
6 cups hot cooked long-grain white rice

Sauté the onion and celery in the margarine in a large saucepan until tender; add the cornstarch and mix thoroughly. Add the stock and cook until smooth and thick; add the tomato juice, Worcestershire, curry powder, and pepper, then the turkey. Heat thoroughly.

Pack the rice into a greased ring mold and let stand in a warm place 10 minutes. Unmold and fill the center with hot curried turkey.

Joe Ginley, retired
Engine 8, F.D.N.Y.

TURKEY AU GRATIN

3 to 4 boneless turkey breasts (1 pound each)
3 bunches broccoli, cut up
1 stick (½ cup) butter
1 cup all-purpose flour
2 cups half-and-half
2 cups milk
1 pound sharp cheddar cheese, grated
1 teaspoon garlic powder
Paprika

Preheat the oven to 350° F.

Roast the turkey 30 to 45 minutes. Cool for 15 minutes, then slice the turkey thin.

Steam the broccoli 4 minutes. Melt the butter in a large pot over very low heat. Add the flour to the melted butter and blend. Cook the mixture for 10 minutes, stirring often to prevent burning. Add the half-and-half, milk, cheese, and garlic powder to the flour mixture; stir until well blended. Allow to cook until the mixture thickens (10 to 15 minutes), stirring often. Add water if necessary (a thick cheese sauce is desired).

Arrange the broccoli spears in a large baking dish. Drape the turkey slices over the broccoli. Pour the cheese sauce over the turkey and broccoli until all is covered. Sprinkle lightly with paprika. Bake, still at 350° F, for 30 to 40 minutes.

Lt. David Loper
Engine 60, F.D.N.Y.

SERVINGS: 10

3 pounds ground turkey
3 medium onions, diced
1 small green bell pepper, diced
½ teaspoon diced garlic
1 can (28 ounces) whole tomatoes
1 can (16 ounces) kidney beans in chili gravy
10½ cups water
2 ounces chili powder
1 beef bouillon cube
1 small jalapeño pepper, split down the middle
½ teaspoon ground cumin
½ teaspoon ground cayenne pepper
½ teaspoon dark brown sugar
4 dashes black pepper
1 tablespoon olive oil
50 strands spaghetti

Brown the turkey in a large pot and break up the large pieces of turkey with a spoon (you don't want the meat too fine). Drain the liquid from the turkey and add the onions, green pepper, and garlic. Cook for 5 minutes (stir to keep from burning).

Add the tomatoes and beans and stir for 2 minutes; this helps to break up the tomatoes.

Add the water, chili powder, bouillon cube, jalapeño pepper, cumin, cayenne pepper, sugar, black pepper, and olive oil.

Bring to a boil, then reduce the heat and cook for 2 hours at a slow boil on low heat.

Add the spaghetti fifteen minutes before serving. Break the spaghetti into small pieces (1 inch long).

Best Batch Turkey Chili is best when not too thin, so you want to cook it until it is thick enough to eat with a fork.

HOW TO EAT THIS: (1) Mainline (AS IS); (2) over spaghetti; (3) over spaghetti with diced onions on top (this is the way I like it); (4) over spaghetti with diced onions and cheese on top (must use Colby longhorn-style cheese).

Gerald L. Newman
Engine Co. 50, Cincinnati, Ohio

DEPUTY CHIEF JOYCE'S ITALIAN TURKEY MEATLOAF

Serve this with pasta and your favorite tomato sauce. It reheats well in sauce.

SERVINGS: 8–10

4 pounds ground turkey
3 cups bread crumbs
3 large eggs
½ cup skim milk
1½ cups chopped fresh parsley
4 to 6 garlic cloves, finely chopped
½ to 1 cup grated Parmesan or Romano cheese
Salt and pepper to taste
Chopped fresh basil to taste
1 pound fat-free mozzarella cheese, cut into ¾-inch chunks

Preheat the oven to 350° F.

Combine all the ingredients (except the mozzarella) in a large bowl and mix well, using clean hands. Divide the mixture in half.

Lightly spray two loaf pans with no-stick cooking spray. Fill each pan halfway with the turkey mixture and pat down firmly. Press one quarter of the mozzarella chunks randomly into the meat in each pan. Top with the remaining meat (press firmly). Top with the remaining mozzarella cheese.

Bake for approximately 1½ hours. Remove from the oven and let stand for 5 minutes. Remove from the pans and slice.

Deputy Chief Joyce
F.D.N.Y.

Main Courses
Meats

BEEF

Firehouse Pot Roast/*Fell*

Pepper Steak/*Buttino*

Tasty Beef Rollups/*Ruszo*

High Desert Flank Steak/*Lawson*

Tom's Chili/*Killean*

Jim's Chili/*McDonnell*

Mexican Meatloaf/*Hafer*

Mulligan Stew/*Mulligan*

Irish Stew/*Sineno*

Enchilada Casserole/*Day*

Chinese Lobster Sauce/*Fields*

Hamburger Stew/*Malcolm*

Three-Bean Delight/*Henry*

Super Beans/*Harrison*

Sweet and Sour Short Ribs/*Coleman*

VEAL

Veal Scallopini over Noodles/*Cannillo*

Veal Marsala/*Collins*

Veal or Chicken Cordon Bleu/*Sineno*

Veal with Eggplant and Prosciutto, Parmigiana/*Gambino*

Paella/*Gordon*

SAUSAGE AND PORK

Potpourri Richard/*Catapano*

Sausage and Chicken Mélange/*Tortorielle*

Sausage Parmesan/*Flohr*

Sausage and Peppers/*Buttino and Sineno*

Touteire/*Dionne*

A Polish Farewell to Lent/*Kohler*

Potted Pork Chops/*Harris*

Barbecued Spareribs/*Gregorio*

Pork Chops in German Sauce/*Walsh*

Ham, Green Beans, and Potatoes/*Houseal*

Stuffed Fresh Ham/*Sineno*

Sauerbraten/*Bryant*

The Palm Beach Breakfast/*Rhodes*

ETCETERA

Kenny's Vegetarian Dish/*Ruane*

Stuffed Green Bell Peppers with Red Sauce/*Sineno*

Italian Spinach Pie/*Bruno*

Artichoke Pie/*Prince*

"Firemen Do Eat Quiche"/*Walsh*

Savory Rice and Veggies/*Losinno*

Brown Rice Casserole/*Gordon and Sineno*

FIREHOUSE POT ROAST

Serve this with either buttered noodles or mashed potatoes.

SERVINGS: 6

All-purpose flour for dredging
Salt and pepper to taste
3½ to 4 pounds fresh brisket (first cut)
3 tablespoons vegetable oil
⅓ teaspoon dried thyme
½ cup chopped onion
3 garlic cloves, chopped
2 cups canned tomatoes (undrained)
½ teaspoon ground ginger

Mix the flour, salt, and pepper. Dredge the meat in the seasoned flour. Heat the oil in a Dutch oven, add the meat, and brown well on all sides. Pour off the fat.

Add the thyme, onion, and garlic. Stir until the onion begins to brown, then add the tomatoes and ginger. Cover tight and simmer until tender (about 2½ hours).

Remove the meat to a heated platter. Thicken the gravy, if desired, with a little flour mixed with water.

Stanley C. Fell, M.D.
Bureau of Health Services, F.D.N.Y.

SERVINGS: 10–12

6 pounds skirt steak
8 large bell peppers
2 large onions
Vegetable oil
1 cup soy sauce
1 cup cream sherry
1 tablespoon garlic powder
1 tablespoon onion powder
Black pepper to taste
Hot cooked long-grain white rice

Preheat the oven to 400° F.

Cut the skirt steak into bite-size strips. Put in a roasting pan and add enough water to fill half of the pan. Place in the oven till the meat is brown. Remove from the oven, leaving the oven on, and drain off the water; set the meat aside in the roasting pan.

Cut up the peppers and onions and sauté in a little oil in a large frying pan so they remain crisp, not soft. Surround the meat with the peppers and onions. Add the soy sauce, cream sherry, garlic and onion powder, and black pepper. Return the pan to the oven and bake till the meat is cooked, 20 to 30 minutes. Serve over a bed of rice.

Capt. Pat Buttino
Engine 263, F.D.N.Y.

TASTY BEEF ROLLUPS

SERVINGS: 2–3

2 thin slices top round steak, about 8 inches in diameter
8 to 12 ounces sliced baked ham
8 ounces imported Swiss cheese
All-purpose flour
Salt and pepper to taste
Grated Parmesan cheese to taste
2 eggs, beaten
Seasoned bread crumbs
Vegetable oil

Pound the steaks with a meat mallet until very thin. Place 2 to 3 slices of ham on each steak to cover. Then place 2 to 3 slices Swiss cheese on top of the ham. Take one end of the beef and begin to roll up, being careful to keep the ham and cheese in place. Coat each roll with flour mixed with salt, pepper, and grated Parmesan cheese. Dip in beaten egg, and then roll each in seasoned bread crumbs.

In a large skillet, heat enough oil to cover the bottom of the pan. Place the meat in the pan and cook slowly, 20 to 25 minutes. Turn the pieces every few minutes to brown them evenly.

Preheat the oven to 375° F.

After 25 minutes, cut each roll into 1-inch-thick slices and place in a shallow baking dish. Bake about 10 minutes. This will finish cooking all the meat and will melt the cheese. Gravy rendered can be used over rice or noodles.

Capt. Robert Ruszo
Oneonta Fire Dept., Oneonta, New York

Serve with salad and baked potato for guaranteed success. Leftovers (if any) make great sandwiches.

SERVINGS: 20–24

10 pounds flank steak
3 cups vegetable oil
1 to 2 cups soy sauce (to liking)
1½ cups honey
2 tablespoons garlic powder
2 tablespoons ground ginger
¼ cup dehydrated onions
1 can mandarin oranges
1 cup (packed) brown sugar
Juice of ½ lemon
2 or 3 green onions
½ garlic clove, crushed

Cut the meat into steak-size pieces for BBQ. Set aside. Mix the remaining ingredients in a container with lid suitable for marinating (e.g., Tupperware; onions will prevail in your fridge if not airtight). Be sure the container is large enough for all the meat. It may be necessary to mix all the ingredients (*except the meat!*) in a pot and allow to simmer only enough to melt the brown sugar and honey. Allow to cool before introducing the meat. Taste and add more honey and brown sugar, if desired. Marinate overnight. BBQ only for maximum flavor. Slice in thin slices at an angle against the grain.

Peter Lawson
Engine 311, Victorville, California

My editor on the original *Firefighter's Cookbook* asked me to come down to the office to look at some recipes prior to a TV appearance I would be making for the first cookbook and to get my opinion on recipes she had selected. I asked if she had included the recipes from the two deceased firefighters that I had submitted. She said that she was sorry, but that she had forgotten all about it. She apologized again, saying that I had given her a lot of recipes and that she would find them and put them in. We continued our discussions about the recipes, and she said that, of them, the most I had given her were chilies, and that she had selected two of them, because they were so different, and that it was the only double in the book.

When I had gone to the widows for recipes, one gave me a dozen (little did I know that she was a caterer), and the other went to her husband's firehouse and got a couple of recipes that he was famous for cooking. Now here I am, in my editor's office looking through the pages of the manuscript, and I hit the chili recipes, and I said, "I don't believe what I'm seeing." The editor asked what I meant. I said, "Well, these are the two deceased firefighters." She said, "Well, that's great." I said, "I know it's great, but I just don't believe it. Here you tell me I gave you an awful lot of recipes for chilies, and one widow gives me a dozen recipes, the other gives me only a few, but you picked these two chilies, and it's the only double in the book, side by side. Here's two firefighters who died in two different incidents, two weeks apart, in the Bronx. They both came from the same town of Mahopac, New York, they were both laid out in the same funeral home, they were both buried at a mass from the same church, and they were both buried in the same cemetery. And they were the only two side by side in my book of a double recipe. If the man upstairs is picking them, then we have a winner."

John Sineno

TOM'S CHILI

SERVINGS: 5–6

2½ pounds ground beef
1 teaspoon adobo seasoning
1 can okra, drained
½ teaspoon salt
½ teaspoon pepper
1½ teaspoons chili powder
2 cans (4 ounces each) mushrooms, chopped
1 green bell pepper, chopped
1 onion, chopped
1 large can crushed tomatoes
1 large can kidney beans
5 dashes hot pepper sauce
1 can (15 ounces) pinto beans

Brown the meat in a skillet and drain off the fat. Put meat in a 4-quart pot and add 2 cups water. Add the remaining ingredients. Simmer over low heat for 2 hours. Keep the pot covered. Stir occasionally.

Tom Killean
Ladder 55, F.D.N.Y.

JIM'S CHILI

SERVINGS: 6–8

1 pound mild Italian sausage, skinned and crumbled
1 pound ground beef chuck
1 large onion, diced
2 large garlic cloves, minced
1½ tablespoons chili powder, or to taste
1 can (6 ounces) tomato paste
1½ cups water
1 tablespoon instant coffee
1 tablespoon sugar
1 tablespoon paprika
1 tablespoon dried oregano
1 teaspoon salt
1 teaspoon pepper
1 teaspoon ground cumin
1 cup dark red kidney beans, drained
1 cup refried beans
Grated Monterey Jack cheese and finely chopped green onions

Brown the sausage, ground chuck, onion, and garlic in a large skillet or pot. Add the remaining ingredients except the beans, bring to a boil, cover, and simmer for 1¼ hours.

While the meat mixture is cooking, combine the kidney and refried beans; set aside. After the meat is cooked, add the beans and stir. Top with Monterey Jack cheese and finely chopped green onions.

Capt. James F. McDonnell
Engine 81, F.D.N.Y.

MEXICAN MEATLOAF

SERVINGS: 6–8

1½ pounds ground beef (turkey and/or chicken may be substituted)
1 package (10 ounces) frozen corn niblets, thawed
1 bunch fresh coriander, chopped
1 jar salsa
1 onion, chopped
1 cup tortilla chips, pulverized
1 package (10 ounces) frozen chopped spinach, thawed (optional)

Preheat the oven to 350° F.

Thoroughly mix together all the ingredients. Pack into a loaf pan and bake 1 to 1½ hours until done.

Carol B. Hafer
Former Counsel, F.D.N.Y.

MULLIGAN STEW

SERVINGS: 8

4 pounds stew beef
Salt and pepper to taste
½ cup all-purpose flour
⅔ cup cubed carrots
1 cup cubed turnips
1 small onion, cut in thin slices
4 cups peeled and sliced potatoes
¼ cup cold water

Cut the meat into 1½-inch cubes. Sprinkle with salt and pepper and dredge in ¼ cup of the flour. Grease a frying pan, add the meat, and stir constantly to sear all surfaces quickly. When well browned, put in a large saucepan. Rinse the frying pan with boiling water and pour over the meat to cover. Boil 5 minutes. Reduce the heat and simmer, covered, until the meat is tender (3 hours for lesser cuts).

Add the carrots, turnips, onion, salt, and pepper for the last hour of cooking. One half hour before the stew is done, skim off the fat and add the potatoes. Thicken with the remaining ¼ cup flour mixed with ¼ cup cold water. Cook an additional 5 minutes.

Assistant Commissioner John Mulligan
F.D.N.Y.

SERVINGS: 4

1 pound boneless lamb, cubed
1 pound boneless beef, cubed
1 medium onion, chopped
2 tablespoons vegetable oil
8 cups boiling water
1 large can tomato sauce
5 medium carrots, peeled and cut in half
6 medium potatoes, peeled and quartered
1 bay leaf
Salt and pepper to taste
1 can (11 ounces) corn niblets or string beans (optional), drained

Brown the lamb, beef, and onions in the oil in a large saucepan. Add the boiling water and tomato sauce to the meat; simmer, covered, 1 hour. Add the carrots, potatoes, bay leaf, salt, and pepper; cook until the carrots and potatoes are done. If using, add the corn niblets and/or string beans during the last 5 minutes. Remove the bay leaf before serving.

John Sineno, retired
Engine 58, F.D.N.Y.

ENCHILADA CASSEROLE

This tastes great rewarmed in the microwave next day.

SERVINGS: 4

2 pounds ground beef
2 cans enchilada sauce (mild or hot)
Dash each of salt and pepper
Dash each of dried thyme and basil
1 small onion, grated
1 package tortillas (12 in package), thawed if frozen
2 or 3 cups grated sharp or extra-sharp cheddar cheese

Preheat the oven to 350° F.

Brown the beef in a skillet and drain off the fat. Add both cans of sauce, salt and pepper, thyme and basil, and the grated onion. Let simmer on low heat about 10 minutes. Do not cover.

In a square baking dish, put a layer of 4 tortillas. Spoon a third of the beef mixture over this layer and sprinkle with a third of the grated cheese. Add another layer of 4 tortillas and repeat the beef mixture and cheese. Do this again for a third layer.

Cover and bake until the cheese is melted (about 15 to 20 minutes). Serve hot.

Chief H. Lee Day III
Monelison Volunteer Fire Department, Madison Heights, Virginia

Serve this on a bed of white rice, topped off with pieces of lobster, crab, or shrimp. It's also excellent on boiled noodles.

SERVINGS: 4–6

2 pounds ground beef
2 eggs, beaten
4 beef bouillon cubes
2 tablespoons sugar
2 tablespoons soy sauce
¼ cup Chinese brown sauce (see note)
4 tablespoons cornstarch
2 cups hot water
2 garlic cloves, sliced, or 1 tablespoon garlic powder

Brown the beef in a skillet and drain off the fat. Add the beaten eggs and scramble the eggs and meat together well. Add the bouillon cubes, sugar, soy sauce, brown sauce, and cornstarch to the hot water; mix well, making sure that cornstarch is dissolved. Immediately pour over the meat mixture and blend well. Add the garlic and simmer 10 minutes, uncovered.

NOTE: You can find Chinese brown sauce with the soy sauce at the market; it looks like molasses.

W. Fields
Boston Engine 5, East Boston, Massachusetts

HAMBURGER STEW

This is a great one for those cold and rainy days!

SERVINGS: ENOUGH FOR AN ARMY OF HUNGRY FIREMEN!

3½ to 4 pounds lean ground beef
2½ to 3 cups water
3 cans (16 ounces each) tomato sauce
2 cans (6 ounces) tomato paste
5 large potatoes, peeled and chopped into ¼-inch pieces
3 cans corn niblets, drained
2 large celery stalks, roughly chopped
1 large white or yellow onion, roughly chopped
4 large carrots, peeled and sliced into ¼-inch circles
Salt and pepper to taste

Cook the beef in a skillet until browned. Drain off the fat.

Place the meat in a stew pot (extra large, with a lid) along with the water, tomato sauce, tomato paste, potatoes, corn, celery, onion, and carrots. Season with salt and pepper.

Mix well. Cover with the lid and simmer on medium-low heat until the potatoes are cooked all the way through (about 2 hours).

Serve nice and hot.

SN Carrie Malcolm
Governors Island Fire Department, Governors Island, New York

You can't screw this one up! The longer it sits, the better it gets.

SERVINGS: 12

1 pound ground beef
1 pound bacon
1 large onion, chopped
½ cup ketchup
½ cup (packed) brown sugar
½ cup barbecue sauce
¼ cup prepared mustard
¼ cup molasses
1 teaspoon chili powder
1 teaspoon pepper
2 cans (16 ounces each) red kidney beans
2 cans (16 ounces each) butter beans
2 cans (16 ounces each) baked beans

Preheat the oven to 350° F.

Brown the ground beef in a skillet and drain off the fat. Put the beef in an ovenproof casserole. Fry the bacon in the skillet until crisp; crumble and add to beef. Drain off most of the bacon fat from the skillet; and the onion to the skillet and sauté. Add to the beef and bacon.

Add all the other stuff to the mixture, stir, and bake for 1 hour. Stir occasionally.

Kenneth C. Henry
Hillsborough County Fire Department, Brandon, Florida

SUPER BEANS

I found this recipe in a *Firehouse* magazine and modified the ingredients slightly. I also recommend serving the beans as my mother did—on top of buttered bread. The Harrington Park Fire Department has two men cook for each of our 24 yearly drills. When my name appears on the list, people ask, "Are you going to serve those beans again?"

SERVINGS: 24

1 pound ground beef
1 can (50 ounces) baked beans
1 envelope dry onion soup
1 cup water
¼ cup (packed) brown sugar
1 bottle (12 ounces) ketchup
½ cup cider vinegar
1 loaf bread (24 slices)
1 stick (½ cup) butter or margarine

Fry the beef in a heavy frying pan until it is browned. While you are doing this, warm up the beans in a large pot and add the other ingredients, stirring to make sure they are thoroughly mixed in. Add the beef, cover the pot, and simmer for 30 to 45 minutes. While it is simmering, butter the slices of bread.

To serve, spoon a ladleful of the mixture onto a slice of bread.

Richard Harrison
Harrington Park Co. #1, Harrington Park, New Jersey

SERVINGS: 6

3 to 3½ pounds beef short ribs
⅓ cup plus 2 tablespoons all-purpose flour
3 tablespoons vegetable oil or butter
⅛ teaspoon pepper
1½ cups sliced onions
2 garlic cloves, sliced
1 bay leaf
2 cups hot water
½ cup vinegar
1 cup ketchup
½ teaspoon salt
2 tablespoons water
Hot buttered noodles

Cut the short ribs into serving pieces; remove excess fat. Dredge the ribs in the ⅓ cup flour and place in a frying pan. Brown well on all sides in the oil, then remove to a heavy pot. Add the pepper, onions, and garlic to the fat in the skillet and cook until tender; add to the short ribs along with the bay leaf. Combine the hot water, vinegar, ketchup, and salt and pour over the ribs. Cover tightly and cook slowly until tender, 2½ to 3 hours.

Remove the ribs to a serving platter and keep warm. Skim off the fat from the gravy; stir in the 2 tablespoons flour mixed with the 2 tablespoons water.

Serve on hot buttered noodles.

Deputy Chief William J. Coleman
Chief in Charge, Bureau of Health Services, F.D.N.Y.

VEAL SCALLOPINI OVER NOODLES

SERVINGS: 6–8

2 cans (13 ounces each) chicken broth
2 small cans tomato sauce
1½ tablespoons Gravy Master
1 tablespoon dried basil
2 pounds veal scallopini
1 pound fresh mushrooms, sliced
3 garlic cloves, chopped
2 tablespoons butter
⅓ cup sherry
Chopped fresh parsley
Hot cooked broad noodles

Preheat the oven to 375° F.

In a saucepan, bring the broth, tomato sauce, Gravy Master, and basil to a boil. Pour over the veal in a baking dish and cover with foil. Bake for 1 hour.

Just before the veal is cooked, sauté the mushrooms and garlic in the butter until golden brown; add the sherry and parsley to taste. Pour over the veal.

Serve over broad noodles.

NOTE: If desired, you can thicken the sauce with cornstarch.

Lawrence Cannillo, retired
Engine 82 and Ladder 31, F.D.N.Y.

VEAL MARSALA

SERVINGS: 3

¼ cup grated Parmesan cheese
2 tablespoons all-purpose flour
Pepper
1 pound veal, thinly sliced and pounded
½ stick (¼ cup) butter
1 can (8 ounces) sliced mushrooms, drained
1 cup beef broth
2 tablespoons Marsala wine

Mix the cheese, flour, and pepper and set aside.

Cut the veal into 2- or 3-inch pieces. Brown the veal in the butter in a skillet; add the mushrooms and brown. Blend in the cheese mixture. Add beef broth and wine, cover, and cook over low heat for 30 minutes, or until the meat is tender. Uncover and cook until the sauce is the desired consistency.

Fireman Jerry Collins
Brooklyn/Queens Holy Name Society

Firefighting Family

I'll be sitting in the firehouse and I'll get a call from a fireman. He's calling me up asking me how to cook something because he invited some young lady to his apartment, not because he's cheap, but because he feels more comfortable. He's asking me how I can help him impress this young lady . . . and now *I'm* impressed. I give him a recipe.

I see him a week later and he's smiling, so I guess I did something right

John Sineno

VEAL OR CHICKEN CORDON BLEU

SERVINGS: 12

8 ounces sliced boiled ham
8 ounces sliced Swiss cheese
12 veal or chicken cutlets, thinly sliced
1 cup all-purpose flour
1½ cups bread crumbs
2 eggs, beaten
Vegetable oil

Preheat the oven to 400° F.

Cut the ham and cheese into wide strips. Lay out the cutlets on your countertop. Put a strip of ham and cheese on each cutlet, then roll tight. Add a toothpick to hold together, if needed.

Use three bowls, one for flour, one for bread crumbs, and one for the eggs. Roll the meat in the flour, then in the egg, then in the bread crumbs. Put a little oil in a frying pan and fry the rolled meat until browned on all sides. Place sautéed rolls in a baking pan and bake for about 20 minutes.

John Sineno, retired
Engine 58, F.D.N.Y.

VEAL WITH EGGPLANT AND PROSCIUTTO, PARMIGIANA

SERVINGS: 4–6

2–3 eggs
⅔ cup milk
2 cups bread crumbs
1 pound thin veal cutlets
Olive oil
1 medium-size eggplant
1 jar (32 ounces) spaghetti sauce
4 to 8 ounces thinly sliced prosciutto ham (trim off fat)
1 pound mozzarella cheese, grated
Chopped fresh parsley

Preheat the oven to 350° F.

Beat the egg and milk in a bowl. Dip the veal in the milk and egg mixture, then roll in the bread crumbs; then place in a frying pan with hot olive oil and fry briefly, 2 to 3 minutes each side. Remove and reserve.

Slice the eggplant lengthwise ¼ inch thick and fry in more hot oil in the skillet till firm yet tender. Place on paper towels and drain off excess oil.

Cover the bottom of a baking pan with some spaghetti sauce and arrange the cutlets over it. Top each cutlet with a slice each of eggplant and prosciutto. Pour more sauce over them generously, using the rest of the sauce over pasta. Top the cutlets with grated mozzarella and sprinkle with chopped fresh parsley. Bake for 20 to 30 minutes.

Frank Gambino
Engine 58, F.D.N.Y.

SERVINGS: 4

2 tablespoons olive oil
4 links sweet sausage (you can use hot sausage, if desired)
1 pound chicken pieces (legs and thighs)
1 each green and red bell pepper, cut in small pieces
1 cup finely chopped onion
1 garlic clove, chopped
Saffron to taste
1 large bay leaf
1 dried hot red pepper (optional)
½ teaspoon dried thyme
1 cup undrained canned tomatoes
1 cup long-grain white rice
¾ cup water
Salt and pepper to taste
8 to 12 littleneck clams
8 to 12 shrimp, shelled and deveined
8 ounces scallops, optional

Heat the oil in a large deep skillet. Prick the sausages with a fork and cook in the hot oil about 5 minutes, turning often. Add the chicken pieces, skin side down, and continue cooking until the sausages and chicken are thoroughly cooked, 15 to 20 minutes.

Add the peppers, onion, and garlic to the skillet. Stir in the saffron, bay leaf, dried red pepper, and thyme. Add the tomatoes, rice, water, salt, and pepper. Cover tightly and cook 15 minutes. Add the clams, shrimp, and scallops to the rice mixture. Cover again and let cook about 8 minutes more.

Lt. Norman Gordon
Engine 304, F.D.N.Y.

You may add or use other vegetables of your choice here. If you want to make Potpourri Richard Supreme, just add shrimp.

SERVINGS: 8

Olive oil
2 pounds Italian sausage, cut into bite-size pieces
1 pound skinless, boneless chicken breast, cut into bite-size pieces
1 head broccoli, cut up
1 head cauliflower, cut up
2 pounds potatoes, peeled and cut into bite-size pieces
1 package instant onion soup, mixed with a little hot water
1 to 1½ pounds London broil
1 small onion, chopped
8 ounces fresh mushrooms, cut in half if large
1 tablespoon chopped fresh parsley
2 garlic cloves, chopped
3 shakes Worcestershire sauce

Coat a frying pan with oil and heat. Brown the sausage, chicken, broccoli, cauliflower, and potatoes, in that order, in the frying pan, placing each item as it is cooked in a flameproof casserole. If necessary, add more oil while browning. Place the casserole on low heat and stir in the instant onion soup mixed with a little hot water.

Broil or barbecue the beef while frying the other items. When the steak is cooked, cut it up into strips and add to the casserole. Any juice from the steak should be added to the casserole.

Sauté the onion, mushrooms, parsley, and garlic in more oil in the frying pan until the onion is soft. Add the Worcestershire sauce and pour the mixture into the casserole. (If more juice is needed, add hot water.)

Tony Catapano
Engine 202, F.D.N.Y.

SAUSAGE AND CHICKEN MÉLANGE

I did a lot of cooking as a firefighter, less as a lieutenant, and even less as a captain. I cooked this meal one night as captain of Ladder 119, Williamsburg, Brooklyn. Before we could eat, we responded to a fire alarm in a factory building. Rescue 2 was already at the fire. Naturally, they left before we did. When we finally returned to quarters, we found a note on the kitchen table thanking us for a good meal. It was signed Rescue 2.

SERVINGS: 16–20

½ cup olive oil
7 pounds medium potatoes, peeled and cut in eighths
3 pounds large green bell peppers, sliced in eighths
4 medium onions, sliced
2 tablespoons dried oregano
Salt and pepper to taste
4 broiling chickens, cut up
6 pounds Italian sausage (sweet or hot, as desired)

Preheat the oven to 350° F.

Pour the olive oil into a roasting pan. Alternate layers of potatoes, peppers, and onions in the pan, seasoning with some of the oregano and salt and pepper to taste. Place the chicken parts on top and season as above. Place the sausages on top of chicken parts and season as above. (Juice from the sausages will seep down through the other ingredients.) Bake, uncovered, for about 1½ hours. Check periodically and turn the ingredients as needed.

Chief Adolph S. Tortorielle, retired
Support Service, F.D.N.Y.

SAUSAGE PARMESAN

Serve this over vermicelli (thin spaghetti), with garlic bread and tossed salad. This one should keep them warm and happy for quite a while.

Enjoy!

SERVINGS: 4

2 pounds unspiced bulk pork sausage (substitute mildly spiced or hot spiced sausage if you prefer; see note)
½ teaspoon salt (unnecessary if spiced sausage is used)
1 teaspoon pepper (unnecessary if spiced sausage is used)
1 teaspoon paprika (unnecessary if spiced sausage is used)
1 teaspoon chopped garlic (unnecessary if spiced sausage is used)
1 cup cracker meal or bread crumbs (optional)
1 jar (32 ounces) of your favorite spaghetti sauce
4 slices mozzarella or provolone cheese
1 pound vermicelli (i.e., thin spaghetti)

Preheat the oven to 350° F.

Mix the spices and sausage together and form 4 sausage patties.

Fry the patties in a skillet over a medium-hot flame until brown on the outside, using your spatula occasionally to press on the patties in order to remove excess grease. (The patties can be breaded prior to frying if you prefer.)

After the patties are browned and drained, and the fat is drained from the skillet, return the patties to the skillet, add the spaghetti sauce, and bake for half an hour.

Remove the skillet from the oven and place a slice of cheese on top of each hot patty. Let the cheese melt slightly.

NOTE:This recipe can easily be increased for any number of people by adding ½ pound of sausage per person.

Lester A. Flohr
Company 12, Dayton, Ohio

SAUSAGE AND PEPPERS

SERVINGS: 12–16

6 pounds Italian sausage
8 bell peppers, cubed
2 large onions, chopped
1 cup soy sauce
1 tablespoon garlic powder
1 tablespoon onion powder
Black pepper

Preheat the oven to 400° F.

Put the sausage in a roasting pan and add enough water to cover the bottom of the pan. Bake for 30 minutes, or until sausage is golden brown. Remove from the oven, leaving the oven on, and drain the fat from the pan and the sausages on paper towels.

Cook the peppers and onions till tender in water to cover. Drain, reserving 1 cup water.

Cut the sausages into bite-size pieces and return to the pan. Add the soy sauce to the pan along with 1 cup water from the peppers and onions. Pour the drained peppers and onions over the sausage and add garlic and onion powder and black pepper to taste. Return to the oven for an additional 15 minutes.

Capt. Pat Buttino
Engine 263, F.D.N.Y.

John Sineno, retired
Engine 58, F.D.N.Y.

TOUTEIRE

(Traditional French-Canadian Pork Pie)

SERVINGS: 8–12

Pastry dough for two 9-inch, two-crust pies
3 pounds lean ground pork
2 cups water
2 large onions, thinly sliced or chopped
6 medium potatoes, cooked and mashed
2 tablespoons salt
1½ tablespoons dried sage
½ tablespoon ground cinnamon
¼ tablespoon ground cloves

Prepare the pastry dough and line two 9-inch pie plates.

Cook the ground pork in the water for about 1 hour, then drain off the excess water and fat.

Preheat the oven to 350° F.

Combine the pork with the remaining ingredients, then divide between the two pie plates. Cover with the top crusts, flute the edges, and bake for 1 hour.

Nelson Dionne
Car 21, Salem, Massachusetts

A POLISH FAREWELL TO LENT

Serve this with horseradish or mustard.

SERVINGS: 14 (OR 7 FIREFIGHTERS)

5 pounds fresh kielbasa (not smoked)
5 pounds sauerkraut

Place the kielbasa in a large pot and cover with water. Bring to a boil and simmer for 45 minutes, then add the sauerkraut and continue to simmer for 30 minutes.

Deputy Commissioner James E. Kohler
F.D.N.Y.

POTTED PORK CHOPS

SERVINGS: 2

1 onion, finely chopped
2 tablespoons butter
4 pork chops
3 cups water
1 package brown gravy mix
8 ounces large egg noodles, cooked

Brown the onions in butter in a skillet. Add the pork chops and brown on both sides. Add the water and brown gravy mix. Cover and let simmer for 45 minutes to 1 hour, until the meat is tender. Serve over a bed of noodles.

Fireman Jim Harris
Brooklyn/Queens Holy Name Society

SERVINGS: 12

8 pounds spareribs (cut into individual portions)
2 sticks (1 cup) margarine
4 onions, chopped or cut into small pieces
2 cups water
1 cup ketchup
¼ cup vinegar
⅓ cup Worcestershire sauce
1 tablespoon prepared mustard
1 teaspoon pepper

Preheat the oven to 400° F.

Brown the individual servings of ribs, in batches, in a large frying pan. Pour out the fat drippings. Melt the margarine in the same frying pan and add the onions. Sauté for 2 minutes. Put the spareribs and onions in a large baking pan. Mix all the other ingredients in a saucepan and cook for about 2 minutes, stirring often. Pour over the ribs, mix well, and cover the pan with aluminum foil. Bake for about 2 hours.

James J. Gregorio
Engine 315, F.D.N.Y.

Serve this with applesauce flavored with cinnamon.

SERVINGS: 8

8 pork chops, about 1 inch thick
3 pounds sauerkraut
2 cups raisins
½ cup honey
1 can (12 ounces) regular beer
1 can (12 ounces) dark beer
1 teaspoon dried sage
1 teaspoon tarragon
2 teaspoons parsley flakes
½ teaspoon black pepper

Brown the pork chops in a little oil in a large deep skillet. Add the remaining ingredients and cook, covered, for 30 minutes.

Fire-Medic Eugene T. Walsh, Jr.
Engine 54, F.D.N.Y.

HAM, GREEN BEANS, AND POTATOES

Serve this with Italian bread and butter. Some of our guys like to add vinegar to the dish, which gives it a different flavor.

SERVINGS: 8–12

1 piece of ham (3 to 4 pounds), with or without knuckle
2 medium onions
5 pounds potatoes
3 pounds fresh green beans, trimmed (or substitute frozen cut green beans)
Salt and pepper

Cut up the ham in small chunks and place with water to cover in a 3- or 4-gallon pot.

Boil off fat (for the more health-conscious, you can trim off the fat, but it won't give you a rich broth) to make a rich broth for about an hour or so.

Peel the onions and potatoes and cut in 1-inch chunks, then add to the ham and broth. Boil until the potatoes are almost soft.

Add the green beans and simmer for about 15 to 20 minutes. Add salt and pepper to taste.

Dave Houseal
Station 2, B Platoon, Harrisburg, Pennsylvania

STUFFED FRESH HAM

SERVINGS: 8–12 (DEPENDING ON SIZE OF HAM)

1 fresh ham (13 to 18 pounds) with a pocket for stuffing
4 to 16 links Italian sausage

Preheat the oven to 400° F.

Put the ham in a roasting pan and surround with water. Bake for about 2 hours. Remove from the oven, leaving the oven on.

Strip the sausage from the casings and stuff the pocket in the ham with the sausage meat. Add more water to pan if needed, then return to the oven till the ham is cooked, about 1 hour longer.

NOTE: When the ham is done, drain off the juices from the roasting pan and put into another container. Place in the refrigerator for at least ½ hour. Remove the fat that rises to the top and use the juices to make pork gravy.

John Sineno, retired
Engine 58, F.D.N.Y.

SAUERBRATEN

SERVINGS: 12–14

5 to 8 pounds venison roast
2 tablespoons pickling spices
½ cup sugar
Salt and pepper
1 quart cider vinegar
4 onions, chopped

Place all the ingredients in a large pot. Cover with 1 inch of water and refrigerate, covered, for 3 to 4 days. Pour the juice out and save. Brown meat and onions in the pot, then pour the juice in, one cup at a time, and cook, uncovered, till all is evaporated, about 2 hours.

Joe Bryant
Rescue 3, F.D.N.Y.

Served with biscuits, this makes a good Southern breakfast for firefighters with a hearty appetite.

SERVINGS: ENOUGH FOR 5–7 FIREFIGHTERS

1 pound sausage, removed from casings
3 potatoes, diced (see note)
1 small onion, diced
1 small green bell pepper, diced
1 dozen jumbo eggs
¼ teaspoon chopped garlic
Pepper to taste
3 slices cheese

Cook the sausage in a skillet and drain on paper towels. Drain off the fat from the skillet, add the diced potatoes, onion, and green pepper to the skillet, and sauté. Beat the eggs in a large bowl; add the garlic and pepper and mix.

Return the sausage to the vegetables in the skillet and pour the eggs over. Mix, then cook on medium heat until thick. Lay the cheese slices on top and cook, covered, until the cheese is melted. Serve just like a pie.

NOTE: You may use 8 ounces potatoes O'Brien from the freezer section of your store.

Paramedic Rick Rhodes
Reserve 11, Battalion 1, Stuart, Florida

It was late November in 1970. I was just a new probie assigned to Ladder 26. Traditionally, in the firehouse at that time, the pre-diet era, everyone was in on the meal. I don't know how many vegetarians there were on the job at the time, but I was sure I was the only one. It was still very weird not to eat meat back then. For my first few tours I didn't eat anything, but that didn't work because I was starving. So finally one night I got up the nerve to bring in my own meal and had the audacity to cook it on John Sineno's stove. I was nervous about everyone ribbing me, so I started cooking early. Then Sineno came in and took a look at what I was cooking. I waited for the sneers, but they didn't come. John just started asking me, "What's this, what's that, and what the hell are you going to do with all these almonds?"

It was my first meeting with John Sineno, Head Chef at Engine 58 and Ladder 26. Other fellows cooked, but John was the *chef.* He made me feel great that night, and we became friends. Whenever I cooked, he always asked me what I was making. Even until today I wish I could have jumped in on John's aromatic, delicious-looking, but unfortunately nonvegetarian meals. John was always calling to me, "Plenty of salad, Kenny—do you want any?"

John never ceased to amaze me. Whether cooking for ten, twenty, thirty, or a hundred, he always seemed to be having a good time. His little philosophical quips, which I called Sinenoisms, were my after-dinner mints. "Chef" John Sineno is definitely one of the legends in firehouse tales.

Kenny Ruane
Ladder 16, F.D.N.Y.

KENNY'S VEGETARIAN DISH

SERVINGS: 3

1 to 2 tablespoons safflower oil
1 onion, sliced
1 green bell pepper, sliced
¼ head cabbage, thinly sliced
1 small head broccoli, chopped
1 cup mung bean sprouts
½ cup raw almonds
1 cup brown rice, cooked
Tamari soy sauce

Lightly cover a pan with safflower oil and sauté the onion and pepper. Add the cabbage and broccoli and sauté till tender. Add bean sprouts and almonds. Toss. Serve over cooked brown rice with Tamari soy sauce.

Kenny Ruane
Ladder 16, F.D.N.Y.

STUFFED GREEN PEPPERS WITH RED SAUCE

SERVINGS: 12

Peppers:
6 to 7 cups cooked long-grain white rice
1 jar olive condite
Garlic powder
Salt and pepper
Dried basil to taste
Parsley flakes to taste
12 green bell peppers, tops removed and seeded
Vegetable oil

Red Sauce:
1 small onion, chopped
2 garlic cloves, minced
2 tablespoons vegetable oil
2 cans whole tomatoes
Salt and pepper to taste
Dried basil to taste
Parsley flakes to taste

Combine the rice, condite, garlic powder, salt, pepper, basil, and parsley. Set aside.

Parboil the peppers in simmering water, drain, and let cool. Fill each one with some of the rice mixture. Heat some oil in a frying pan and quickly sauté the peppers, in batches on all sides. Turn the peppers upside down and fry the tops just enough to brown the stuffing.

For the red sauce, sauté the onion and garlic in the oil in a saucepan. Core the tomatoes and add to the pan. Add salt and pepper, basil, and parsley. Simmer 45 minutes, then set aside for 30 to 60 minutes.

Meanwhile, preheat the oven to 350° F. Set the peppers straight up in a roasting pan. Pour the sauce over the peppers and bake for about ½ hour, or until the peppers are soft.

John Sineno, retired
Engine 58, F.D.N.Y.

Perhaps the saddest occasion I cooked for was Larry Fitzpatrick's funeral.

Larry and I had worked together for years. He then transferred to Rescue 3. He died trying to save one of "the brothers."

Fireman Frisby, Ladder 28, was trapped in a blazing room on an upper story of a Harlem tenement. He was able to reach one of the windows and to call for help.

Fitzpatrick went to the roof of the building. He tied a rope around his waist, fastened the other end to a chimney, and went over the side. He lowered himself to the window where Frisby was waiting. Frisby leaned out the window and grabbed Larry. Larry slowly played out the rope as they started down to the alleyway below them.

Then the rope broke.

That night the sad signal 5-5-5-5 announcing the deaths of Fire-fighters Fitzpatrick and Frisby was transmitted to all city fire-houses.

Captain Ryan asked me to do the collation. I had to feed the thousands of firefighters who attended Larry's funeral. The Fitz-patricks lived in Merrick, a town on Long Island close to the city, and the Merrick Volunteer Fire Department graciously offered the use of its firehouse for the meal after the services.

Everyone who turned out that day to honor Larry ate a good meal. I didn't eat much myself—the lump in my throat was just too big. We fed over 4,000 people.

John Sineno

ITALIAN SPINACH PIE

SERVINGS: 6

1½ cups thawed frozen spinach
½ stick (¼ cup) butter
Salt and pepper to taste
8 ounces ricotta cheese
3 eggs, lightly beaten
½ cup grated Parmesan cheese
½ cup heavy cream
Ground nutmeg
9-inch pastry shell

Preheat the oven to 375° F.

Cook the spinach in a saucepan with the butter, salt, and pepper; drain thoroughly and place in a bowl. To the spinach add the ricotta cheese, eggs, Parmesan, cream, and nutmeg to taste. Pour the mixture into the pastry shell and bake for 30 minutes, or until the crust is brown and the cheese mixture set.

First Deputy Fire Commissioner Joseph Bruno
F.D.N.Y.

ARTICHOKE PIE

SERVINGS: 6

1 cup diced mozzarella cheese
½ can cut artichokes, diced
½ cup diced pepperoni
¼ cup grated Parmesan cheese
4 eggs, beaten
1 frozen 9-inch pie shell

Preheat the oven to 350° F.

Mix the mozzarella, artichokes, pepperoni, grated cheese, and eggs. Pour into the pie shell and bake 45 to 50 minutes.

Danny Prince
Ladder 156, F.D.N.Y.

SERVINGS: 6

3 cups grated zucchini
1 small onion, chopped
1 cup Bisquick
4 eggs
½ cup vegetable oil
½ cup grated Parmesan cheese
½ teaspoon parsley flakes (¼ cup fresh)
½ teaspoon dried marjoram
¼ teaspoon salt
¼ teaspoon pepper

Preheat the oven to 350° F.

Mix all the ingredients and pour into a large greased pie plate. Bake for 30 minutes, or until golden brown.

Fire-Medic Eugene T. Walsh, Jr.
Engine 54, F.D.N.Y.

SAVORY RICE AND VEGGIES

SERVINGS: 8

Rice:
1 cup long-grain white rice
¼ cup vegetable oil
¾ cup water
1 can (11 ounces) chicken broth
½ teaspoon salt
½ teaspoon pepper
Pinch of cayenne pepper

Veggies:
2 cups broccoli florets
1 cup pitted ripe olives
¼ cup sliced (¼ inch) green onions, green part and all
¼ cup chopped fresh parsley
1 medium tomato, cut into wedges
1 medium green bell pepper, cut into strips
8 ounces summer sausage, halved and sliced ⅛ inch thick

Combine the rice and oil in a 10-inch skillet. Cook over medium heat, stirring occasionally, until the rice is brown (5 minutes). Stir in the water, broth, and seasonings and cook, covered, until the liquid is absorbed (about 15 to 20 minutes).

In a large bowl combine all the vegetables and the sausage. When the rice is done, pour the hot rice over the mixture and toss to mix together.

Joe Losinno
Engine 302, F.D.N.Y.

BROWN RICE CASSEROLE

If you prefer a vegetarian dish, cook the rice in water rather than chicken broth. A splendid, nutritious main dish, about 350 calories per serving.

SERVINGS: 4–5

3 cups chicken broth
1 teaspoon salt
½ teaspoon dried basil
½ teaspoon dried thyme
1 cup brown rice
2 tablespoons vegetable oil
1½ cups (about 8 ounces) diced eggplant
½ cup chopped onion
1 garlic clove, crushed
1 cup (about 4 ounces) sliced zucchini
½ cup chopped green bell pepper
1 medium red bell pepper, diced
1 medium yellow bell pepper, diced
½ cup sliced fresh mushrooms
½ cup chopped broccoli
2 cups (8 ounces) shredded Swiss cheese

In a medium saucepan, bring the chicken broth to a boil. Add the salt, basil, thyme, and rice. Reduce the heat to low and cook, covered, until the liquid is all absorbed, about 45 minutes.

In a large skillet, heat the oil. Add eggplant, onion, garlic, zucchini, peppers, mushrooms, and broccoli. Sauté for 5 minutes, or until tender.

Grease a 2-quart casserole. Preheat the oven to 350° F.

Stir the rice into the vegetables in the skillet. Spoon half the mixture into the casserole and top with half the shredded cheese. Add the remaining rice and vegetables, then top with the remaining cheese. Bake, uncovered, for 35 minutes, or until thoroughly heated through.

Lt. Norman Gordon
Engine 304, F.D.N.Y.

John Sineno, retired
Engine 58, F.D.N.Y.

Vegetables, Salads, AND Side Dishes

Eggplant, Spanish Style/*Santimauro*

Zucchini Casserole/*Ternlund*

Eggplant Rollups/*Sineno*

"Broccoli from Hell"/*Brauchler*

Oriental Stir-Fry Broccoli/*de Meo*

Spinach Balls/*Kessler and Kessler*

Stuffed Artichokes/*Munday*

I Gobbi (Artichoke Stalks)/*Proietti*

"Killer Tomatoes"/*Kessler and Kessler*

The Vegetarian Italian Stallion Casserole/*Tenuto*

Fried Cabbage/*Fargione*

Captain's Cabbage/*Flohr*

Scalloped Potatoes and Onions/*Curry*

Candied Sweet Potatoes/*Sineno*

Wazoo Salad Dressing/*DePinto*

Coleslaw/*Vredenburgh*

Insalata di Carote/*Triozzi*

Insalata dei Pompieri/*Driusi*

German Potato Salad/*Flohr*

Luxembourg Carrots/*Freilinger*

Escarole and Beans/*de Meo*

Cracked Wheat Salad/*McDonnell*

Tortellini Salad/*Ebinger*

Frijoles Negros à la Menocal/*Fonseca*

Fried Rice/*Munday*

Highway Rice/*Prince*

Spanish-Style Rice with Chickpeas/*Granieri*

Joe Lo Cheesy Confetti Rice/*Losinno*

Rice Balls/*Sineno*

Potato Pancakes/*Vredenburgh*

Potato Balls/*Bryant*

Betty's Potato Stuffing/*Suslowitz*

EGGPLANT, SPANISH STYLE

SERVINGS: 8

2 medium eggplants, quartered and boiled until tender
8 eggs, beaten
8 ounces cream cheese
8 ounces farmer cheese
¼ cup grated Italian cheese
Salt and pepper to taste
2 tablespoons butter

Preheat the oven to 350° F.

Scoop out the eggplant (save the skins) and blend with all the remaining ingredients except the butter. Lightly grease a 3-quart round baking dish and line the bottom with the eggplant skins. Pour the eggplant mixture over the skins and dot with the butter. Bake for about 1 hour.

Unmold onto a platter to serve.

Nick Santimauro
Ladder 166, F.D.N.Y.

ZUCCHINI CASSEROLE

SERVINGS: 14

6 pounds fresh zucchini
3 cans (10 ounces each) stewed tomatoes
1 pound sliced Swiss cheese
1¼ cups seasoned bread crumbs

Preheat the oven to 375° F.

Cut the zucchini into ½-inch slices. Parboil in simmering water for approximately 7 minutes (the zucchini is to remain firm). Drain thoroughly.

In a 13 x 9 x 2-inch baking dish, arrange a layer of zucchini, layer of stewed tomatoes, then a single layer of Swiss cheese. Repeat the layers until the zucchini is finished; end with a layer of cheese. Sprinkle with the bread crumbs and bake for 25 minutes.

Stephen Ternlund
Ladder 108, F.D.N.Y.

EGGPLANT ROLLUPS

SERVINGS: 4

1 large eggplant, sliced lengthwise
2 eggs, beaten
1 cup bread crumbs
2 or 3 garlic cloves, finely chopped
2 tablespoons olive oil
15 ounces ricotta cheese
1 small grated mozzarella
1 tablespoon fresh chopped parsley
1 jar (28 ounces) marinara sauce

Preheat the oven to 450° F.

Dip the eggplant slices first in the beaten eggs, then in the bread crumbs, seasoned with the garlic. Brown lightly in oil in a skillet and place on a cutting board. Mix the ricotta, mozzarella, and parsley and spoon a heaping tablespoon of the mixture onto each eggplant slice. Roll up, securing with toothpicks. Arrange in a baking dish and cover with the marina sauce. Bake for 10 to 15 minutes.

John Sineno, retired
Engine 58, F.D.N.Y.

"BROCCOLI FROM HELL"

This dish was dubbed "broccoli from hell" by the members of Engine 326 and Ladder 160 for its assault on the palate. Make sure of a clear path to the water cooler!

SERVINGS: 6

Cloves from 1 head garlic, sliced
6 tablespoons virgin olive oil
4 heads broccoli, cut into florets
1 tablespoon crushed red pepper
¼ teaspoon white pepper
1 teaspoon salt

Sauté the garlic in the oil in a large saucepan until soft. Stir in the broccoli florets and simmer 10 minutes. Add the remaining ingredients and cook until broccoli is al dente, stirring thoroughly. Serve immediately.

Jeff Brauchler
Ladder 160, F.D.N.Y

ORIENTAL STIR-FRY BROCCOLI

SERVINGS: 4

1 bunch broccoli
2 or 3 garlic cloves, chopped
2 to 3 tablespoons vegetable oil
2 tablespoons white wine
3 tablespoons soy sauce
1 teaspoon sugar
Sesame seeds

Cut the broccoli florets off the stalks and set aside. Peel the stalks and cut into thin 2½-inch pieces. Sauté the garlic in the oil in a skillet. Add the stalks and sauté about 1 minute over a high flame. Add the florets, wine, soy sauce, and sugar. Cover, lower the heat, and cook 3 minutes.

Sprinkle with sesame seeds and serve.

Chief of Department Joseph M. de Meo, retired
F.D.N.Y.

SPINACH BALLS

SERVINGS: 2–3

1 package (10 ounces) frozen chopped spinach, thawed and pressed dry
1 garlic clove, minced
½ small onion, minced
¼ cup seasoned bread crumbs
2 large eggs, beaten
2 tablespoons butter, melted and cooled
¼ cup grated Locatelli or Parmesan cheese
10 cubes (½ inch each) mozzarella or ham

Combine all the ingredients except the cubed cheese or ham and refrigerate for 1 hour.

Uniformly shape the spinach mixture into 10 balls slightly larger than the size of a golf ball. Press in one side of each ball so it resembles a small bowl. Insert one cube of mozzarella or ham into each "bowl" and mold the spinach mixture around the cube so the cube becomes the core of the spinach ball.

Place the balls on a lightly greased baking sheet (Pam cooking spray works well for this). Refrigerate for 30 minutes.

Meanwhile, preheat the oven to 350° F.

Remove the baking sheet from the refrigerator and bake the balls, uncovered, for 30 minutes.

NOTE: Preshaped balls may be kept frozen for up to 1 week before baking, but must be thawed for 30 minutes prior to cooking.

Warren William Kessler
Warren G. Kessler, retired
Engine 268, F.D.N.Y.

STUFFED ARTICHOKES

SERVINGS: 6–8

6 medium artichokes
1 small onion, diced
2 garlic cloves, chopped
4 tablespoons vegetable oil
1½ cups seasoned bread crumbs
¼ cup grated Parmesan cheese
Salt and pepper

Cut the stem and top off each artichoke and wash. Pry open and remove the prickly choke. Sauté the onion and garlic in 3 tablespoons oil in a saucepan. When tender, add the bread crumbs, cheese, and salt and pepper. Stuff each artichoke thoroughly and stand up in a pot, adding enough water to cover the bottom half of each artichoke; add the remaining 1 tablespoon oil. Simmer, covered, until tender, about 1 hour.

Jim Munday
Ladder 156, F.D.N.Y.

I was invited to Harry Ahearn's fiftieth anniversary party. It was prior to the publication of the first book, and the publisher had given me about six advance copies. Because Harry had been such a help to me, I wanted to give him one. The young waitress who was serving us saw the books and asked if she could have one. She explained that she was newly married and needed all the help she could get around the kitchen. I told her that the book was not out yet, but that it would be soon.

Later that year I attended a Christmas party at the same restaurant. That same young waitress was serving, and I asked her if she had gotten the book. She said that she had and I offered to autograph it for her. She said that she couldn't because it was all stained and worn from use. We laughed and I thought, what better compliment could I get?

John Sineno

I GOBBI
(ARTICHOKE STALKS)

SERVINGS: 6

6 artichoke stalks
Olive oil
2 cloves garlic, quartered lengthwise
Crushed hot pepper
Salt

Using a potato peeler, peel the artichoke stalks (this recipe calls for the stalks only, not the artichokes). In a pot of salted water, boil the artichoke stalks until they are tender.

Cover the bottom of a frying pan large enough to accommodate the artichoke stalks with olive oil (use only olive oil) and brown the garlic with the hot pepper. Be careful not to burn the garlic. Cut the artichoke stalks into 4 or 5 pieces each. Add to the frying pan and cook over a medium to high flame, stirring occasionally. After about 5 to 8 minutes, serve as a side dish or vegetable.

Assistant Station Chief Bruno Proietti
Engine 7-A Ostiense, Rome, Italy

(Stuffed)

What can be done with that overly productive vegetable garden? Feasting on salads till you're green in the face seems hopeless. And while launching veggies at stock-restrained evildoers in the village square would work, your finding same in this day and age is highly improbable—and catapulting them skyward for target practice would prove extremely messy. Distributing the surplus harvest to everyone you know is, of course, a good solution, but there is however, a finer one. Just keep making these stuffed tomatoes.

Fret not, these tomatoes won't attack, unless a cholesterol or lactose intolerance exists. The expression "killer," without developing calluses from patting myself on the back, denotes that they are exceedingly delicious.

Warren W. Kessler

SERVINGS: 5

5 medium-size firm, ripe tomatoes
Black pepper
3 tablespoons butter or margarine
3 garlic cloves, minced
¼ cup minced onion
1 package (10 ounces) frozen chopped spinach, completely thawed
2½ tablespoons sour cream
1 package (3 ounces) cream cheese, softened and cut into ½-inch cubes
1 cup shredded mozzarella cheese
½ cup grated Parmesan cheese
1 teaspoon chopped fresh basil
½ cup dry bread crumbs, plus additional for topping

Cut the tops off the tomatoes. Using a teaspoon, carefully remove and reserve the pulp. Force pulp through a strainer, rendering at least ½ cup of juice. Lightly sprinkle black pepper inside the tomato shells; invert on paper towels and let drain.

Over low heat, melt 2 tablespoons of the butter or margarine in a skillet. Add the garlic and onion and sauté until soft; set aside.

Place the spinach in the center of an inverted large plate or pie plate. Top with another plate or pie plate of equal proportions. Press together to remove as much of the spinach liquid as possible. Combine the spinach, sour cream, cream cheese, mozzarella, Parmesan, basil, and ½ cup bread crumbs in a food processor; blend thoroughly. If the mixture appears too thin, compensate by gradually adding more bread crumbs; too thick, add more tomato juice. Refrigerate for 30 minutes.

Meanwhile, preheat the oven to 350° F.

Scoop the filling mixture into the reserved tomato shells. Do not overpack. Top with supplementary bread crumbs and dot with bits of the remaining butter. Place in a lightly greased baking dish (see note) and bake for 20 to 30 minutes.

NOTE: Nonreactive cookware should always be used when acidic ingredients are involved. Avoid copper, iron, or aluminum.

Warren William Kessler
Warren G. Kessler, retired
Engine 268, F.D.N.Y.

THE VEGETARIAN ITALIAN STALLION CASSEROLE

You won't believe what your tongue will tell ya. It's that great!

SERVINGS: 4–6

4 large tomatoes, sliced
2 large onions, sliced
Salt and pepper
Season-all
Garlic powder
½ to 1 cup shredded Romano cheese
½ cup Italian seasoned bread crumbs

Preheat the oven to 325° F.

In a 12-inch round casserole dish 2 or 3 inches deep, place a layer of tomatoes on the bottom, then onions, then tomatoes, and then onions again. Finish with a layer of tomatoes on top. At this time place your seasonings on top of the tomatoes, as much or as little as you would like for flavor—salt, pepper, Season-all, garlic powder. After you add your seasonings, put a layer of grated Romano on top of the tomatoes and finish up with a layer of bread crumbs. Bake for 45 minutes to 1 hour, depending on the oven.

John B. Tenuto, Jr.
Orange County Fire Rescue Co., Casselberry, Florida

FRIED CABBAGE

This is delicious with any kind of pork or ham dish.

SERVINGS: 6

1 to 2 pounds cabbage
⅓ cup vegetable oil
6 garlic cloves, minced
2 onions, sliced (optional)
Salt and pepper to taste

Remove any outer leaves of the cabbage that are dirty or bruised. Cut the cabbage in half through the core. Rinse and drain thoroughly. Remove the core and discard. Slice the cabbage lengthwise into ½-inch strips. Set aside.

In a large skillet or wok, heat the oil on medium to high heat and add the garlic. (At this point you can add a couple of sliced onions, if desired.) Sauté the garlic till tender; do not let it brown. Add the cabbage and stir-fry until the cabbage begins to soften. Add salt and pepper and cook until the cabbage is tender but not too soft, about 15 minutes. Do not brown cabbage. You can cook it for more or less time according to the texture you like. Remove from the heat and serve.

Carl J. Fargione
Engine 309, F.D.N.Y.

CAPTAIN'S CABBAGE

This recipe was given to me by a captain in our department before he became a chief, proving that all good ideas don't die when you become top honcho!

SERVINGS: 6

1 green bell pepper, cubed
1 medium onion, cubed
1 pound bacon
1 small head cabbage
1 can (28 ounces) peeled tomatoes, drained but juice reserved

Blanch the green peppers and onions in simmering water for 2 to 3 minutes. Drain and set aside.

Cook the bacon until crisp, saving the bacon drippings. Crumble the bacon.

Core the cabbage, cut it up, and place in a large saucepan. Pour the tomato juice over the cabbage. Quarter the peeled tomatoes and add to the cabbage along with the blanched onions and green peppers. Add the saved bacon drippings and cook, covered, over low heat for 20 to 30 minutes. Sprinkle the crumbled bacon over the cabbage and serve it with your meal.

Lester A. Flohr
Company 12, Dayton Fire Department, Dayton, Ohio

SCALLOPED POTATOES AND ONIONS

SERVINGS: 4

5 large potatoes, peeled and sliced thin
¾ cup chopped onion
3 tablespoons butter or margarine
¼ cup all-purpose flour
1¾ cups chicken broth
1½ tablespoons mayonnaise
¾ teaspoon salt
⅛ teaspoon pepper
Paprika

Preheat the oven to 350° F.

In a round casserole dish, layer the potatoes and onions alternately. Set aside.

In a saucepan, melt the butter or margarine and blend in the flour. Gradually stir in the broth, mayonnaise, salt, and pepper. Cook, stirring frequently, until the sauce bubbles and thickens. Pour over the potatoes and sprinkle with paprika. Bake for 1¼ hours.

Capt. Joe Curry
Ladder 26, F.D.N.Y.

CANDIED SWEET POTATOES

SERVINGS: 6

6 large sweet potatoes
¼ cup Kahlúa liqueur
Miniature marshmallows

Preheat the oven to 350° F.

Boil the sweet potatoes, then drain, mash, and add the liqueur. Pour into a baking dish and sprinkle with marshmallows. Bake till the marshmallows are melted.

John Sineno, retired
Engine 58, F.D.N.Y.

WAZOO SALAD DRESSING

This salad dressing was thrown together by men working in Ladder 50 in the Bronx and was named Jack McGee Dressing, in honor of his having a small part in *Turk 182* and *Backdraft.* Ladder 116 renamed it Wazoo!

It's great with chef's salad, and if needed it can be cut in half.

SERVINGS: 11

2½ cups olive oil
¼ cup water
½ cup sugar
1⅓ cup wine vinegar
2 teaspoons salt
2 teaspoons pepper
2 teaspoons onion powder
2 teaspoons paprika
2 teaspoons garlic powder
2 teaspoons dry mustard

Combine all the ingredients in a large bowl or pitcher and stir. Chill and serve.

Joseph DePinto, Jr.
Ladder 155, F.D.N.Y.

COLESLAW

SERVINGS: 8–10 (DEPENDING UPON SIZE OF CABBAGE)

1 large head cabbage
2 large carrots, peeled and shredded
1 large green bell pepper, chopped
Mayonnaise
2 to 3 tablespoons white vinegar
Salt and pepper to taste
½ teaspoon sugar

Cut the cabbage in half; core and shred. Mix the cabbage, carrots, and pepper with mayonnaise to the desired consistency. Add the white vinegar and continue to blend. Add salt and pepper, and the sugar. Stir. Refrigerate till well chilled, stirring occasionally.

David Vredenburgh
Engine 248, F.D.N.Y.

INSALATA DI CAROTE

SERVINGS: 6

8 good-size carrots, peeled
½ cup olive oil
Juice of ½ lemon
Salt and pepper

Shred the carrots, add the other ingredients, and let marinate. Serve after a hearty meal. The combination of oil, carotene, and citric acid and sodium forms an exquisitely tasty combination.

Capt. Robert Triozzi
Fire Protection, U.S. Embassy, Rome, Italy

INSALATA DEI POMPIERI
(Firefighter's Salad)

In Italy, salads are served last but prepared first when making a meal. A salad at the end of a meal helps you digest, and preparing it first gives it time to marinate while you enjoy the other four courses that precede it in a normal Italian meal.

Wine is traditionally not served with the salad because salads are usually made with vinegar—and this would upset your palate if you were drinking wine. In fact, the course that follows the salad is cheese, to neutralize your palate so you can resume drinking wine with the *remaining* three courses!

SERVINGS: 6

1 can (16 ounces) cannellini beans
2 carrots, peeled
1 medium fennel bulb
1 leek, well washed
1 small red onion
½ cup olive oil
Salt and pepper
Juice of 1 lemon

Rinse the cannellini in a good amount of water and drain. Chop the carrots, fennel, leek, and onion very fine. Put everything in a salad bowl. Add olive oil, salt, pepper, and lemon juice to taste and let stand to marinate, stirring occasionally.

Station Chief Gilberto Driusi
Engine 12-A, Tuscolano II, Fire Department, Rome, Italy

A Traditional Italian Meal

Capt. Robert Triozzi
Fire Protection, U.S. Embassy, Rome, Italy

Many people ask me what is the line-up for a "traditional Italian meal." Eating is top priority among Italians, and among Italian firefighters in particular. The meal is either what is eaten every day, a semispecial occasion, like a Sunday, or a feast such as Easter, Christmas, or December 4, which is the Feast of Saint Barbara, patron saint of firefighters and celebrated *alla grande* in every firehouse in Italy.

An ordinary meal, eaten around 2 P.M. every day in most Italian homes, is considered *pranzo,* the main meal of the day. It consists of a *primo,* or first course, which is usually pasta or risotto and sometimes polenta (a cornmeal dish made primarily in northern Italy) or gnocchi (Italian potato dumplings popular in Abruzzo). The second course follows and is either meat or fish, after which a salad or vegetable (rarely both) is served, and the pranzo concludes with fresh fruit, whatever happens to be in season.

For a semispecial occasion the meal would begin with an antipasto. This could be a mixed platter of salami, olives, artichokes, etc., or a seafood salad composed of squid, shrimp, mussels, clams, and octopus, or it could be prosciutto and melon or figs (depending on the season). In fact, *antipasto* means before the meal. The antipasto is followed by a *primo,* then a *secondo,* then a vegetable, salad, cheese, and fruit.

A very special occasion is a feast that will occupy most of the day. The surfeit that was enjoyed on the Feast of Saint Barbara in 1988 at fire headquarters in Rome was composed of the following:

1 cold antipasto

1 hot antipasto

Soup

Ravioli filled with ricotta and spinach in tomatoes

Tortellini in a cream sauce

Fettuccine with wild mushrooms

Roast veal

Roast baby lamb

Roast pork

Roast potatoes

Broccoli

Salad

Gorgonzola, provolone, and Bel Paese cheese

Fresh fruit

Panettone (a traditional Italian cake served at Christmas)

Cannoli, cream puffs, sfogliatelle, and other pastries

Espresso coffee and shots of either Sambuca, Amaretto, or grappa

I consider myself quite fortunate to enjoy this feast with my Italian brothers. And I usually sample a different newspaper recipe in Italy every year, since regional cooking varies so much. This meal, by the way, is paid for by the Italian government. It is absolutely free to the firefighters and guests, such as myself and all the retired firefighters that participate as well, along with all the off-duty firemen. This year I will be traveling to Latina, where firefighters will celebrate the Feast of Saint Barbara with firefighters from Germany who are driving their engine down to participate in the festivities.

LUXEMBOURG CARROTS

SERVINGS: 6

1 pound carrots, sliced
½ cup corn oil
¼ cup white wine vinegar
1 teaspoon sugar
½ teaspoon salt
⅛ teaspoon paprika
6 green onions, green part and all, sliced

Boil the carrots until nearly tender. Drain.

In a bowl, combine the oil, vinegar, sugar, salt, and paprika and whisk thoroughly. Add the carrots and green onions and marinate for an hour. Serve hot, at room temperature, or cold as a vegetable or salad. Stir before serving.

J. Joseph Freilinger
West Des Moines Volunteer, Des Moines, Iowa

ESCAROLE AND BEANS
(Italian Soul Food)

SERVINGS: 4

1 head escarole
Olive oil
2 to 3 garlic cloves, sliced
1 large can white kidney beans
Salt and pepper

Wash the escarole thoroughly. Cook in a saucepan with 1 inch of boiling water for 10 to 15 minutes until tender. Drain and rinse under cold water.

Cover the bottom of the pan with oil and sauté the garlic. Add the escarole and fry quickly. Add the beans and salt and pepper to taste. Simmer 15 minutes with the pot partially covered.

Chief of Department Joseph M. de Meo, retired
F.D.N.Y.

GERMAN POTATO SALAD

The dressing for this is a little tough to get right the first time, but when you get a flavor that pleases you, your friends will always be asking you to bring this dish to the picnic!

SERVINGS: 8

1 pound bacon
10 medium potatoes
1 tablespoon salt
¼ cup sugar
1 cup vinegar
1 cup water
½ cup vegetable oil or reserved bacon grease
1 large onion, chopped
Paprika and chopped chives for garnish

Fry the bacon in a skillet. Drain the grease into a cup and save, if desired. Dice the bacon.

Boil the potatoes with the skins on. The potatoes are done when a fork can easily penetrate the potato (approximately ½ hour). Do not overcook! When the potatoes are done, drain them and let them stand in cold water, briefly, in order to cool them off before peeling off the skins from potatoes. After they have cooled and have been peeled, slice them into a large bowl.

Mix the salt, sugar, and vinegar together to make the dressing. Be sure to use a jar to which you have a lid. Taste the mixture. It should not be too salty, vinegary, or sugary. Adjust the flavor by adding more sugar, salt, or vinegar as required to please your palate. Next add water and oil (or bacon grease).

Add the onions and bacon to the sliced potatoes. Put lid on jar in which you made the dressing and shake vigorously. Pour about three quarters of the dressing on top of the potatoes and stir, saving the remaining dressing. The potatoes will absorb the dressing. Check the salad in a couple of minutes to see if the potatoes require more dressing. Add dressing to make the salad as moist as you prefer. Garnish with paprika and chives.

NOTE: Sliced cucumber can also be mixed into the potato salad.

Lester A. Flohr
Company 12, Dayton Fire Department, Dayton, Ohio

CRACKED WHEAT SALAD

(Tabbouleh)

SERVINGS: 4

½ cup fine bulgur (cracked wheat)
2 cups cold water
3 medium tomatoes, diced
½ cup chopped fresh parsley
¼ cup chopped green onions
2 tablespoons chopped fresh mint or 2 teaspoons crumbled dried mint
2 tablespoons olive or salad oil
2 tablespoons lemon juice
1 teaspoon salt
¼ teaspoon ground allspice
¼ teaspoon pepper
Small romaine leaves

About 3 hours before or early in the day, in a bowl combine the bulgur and water and let stand for at least 1 hour. Drain the wheat well, then put in a large bowl. Add the tomatoes and all the remaining ingredients except the romaine leaves. Mix well. Cover and refrigerate for at least 1 hour.

Serve on romaine leaves.

Capt. James F. McDonnell
Engine 81, F.D.N.Y.

TORTELLINI SALAD

SERVINGS: 10–12

8 ounces meat tortellini
8 ounces cheese tortellini
Olive oil
8 ounces fresh green beans, blanched
8 ounces fresh mushrooms, thickly sliced
½ cup black olives, sliced
¾ cup artichoke hearts, quartered
½ cup purple onions, sliced
1 cup chopped sun-dried tomatoes

Dressing:
¾ cup balsamic vinegar
1 cup extra virgin olive oil
1 garlic clove
Salt and black pepper to taste
1½ tablespoons chopped fresh oregano or thyme
1 heaping tablespoon grated Parmesan cheese

Boil the tortellini, rinse, coat lightly with oil, and set aside.

While waiting for the pasta to boil, prepare the green beans, mushrooms, black olives, artichoke hearts, onions, and sun-dried tomatoes.

In a blender, mix the vinegar, olive oil, salt, pepper, oregano, and Parmesan cheese.

Put all the ingredients in a large bowl and mix well. Let stand at room temperature for ½ hour before serving.

Paul M. Ebinger
Governors Island Firehouse, Governors Island, New York

FRIJOLES NEGROS À LA MENOCAL

SERVINGS: 8

¼ cup olive oil
1 onion, diced
1 green bell pepper, diced
4 garlic cloves, crushed
1 can (8 ounces) tomato sauce
3 pinches dried oregano
3 pinches paprika
5 dashes pepper
1 jar (3 ounces) pimientos, drained and diced
3 tablespoons vinegar
2 cans (16 ounces each) black beans

Heat the oil in a frying pan. Add onions, green peppers, and garlic and sauté until tender.

Add the tomato sauce, oregano, paprika, pepper, pimientos, and vinegar. Simmer, uncovered, for 15 minutes, then add the beans, cover, and simmer until the beans are heated through, about 10 minutes.

Capt. William Fonseca
Ladder 165, F.D.N.Y.

FRIED RICE

SERVINGS: 6–8

1½ cups long-grain white rice
3 cups water, lightly salted
10 strips bacon, cut into pieces
1 medium onion, diced
2 eggs, beaten
¼ to ½ cup soy sauce
½ teaspoon garlic powder

Cook the rice in the water according to package directions.

In a large frying pan, cook the bacon until crisp. Remove and drain on paper towels. Cook the onion in bacon grease; add the eggs and stir. Add the bacon and cooked rice to the frying pan; stir in the soy sauce and garlic powder. Cook until the rice is golden brown, stirring occasionally.

NOTE: Bean sprouts, mushrooms, and/or peas can be added for variety.

Jim Munday
Ladder 156, F.D.N.Y.

HIGHWAY RICE

SERVINGS: 10–12

Vinaigrette:
2 tablespoons prepared Dijon-style mustard
½ cup red wine vinegar
2 teaspoons sugar
1 teaspoon salt
1 teaspoon freshly ground pepper
Minced parsley to taste
1 cup imported olive oil

Rice:
8 cups hot cooked rice, as follows:
    2⅔ cups wild rice
    2⅔ cups long-grain white rice
    2⅔ cups brown rice
1 red bell pepper, finely chopped
1 green bell pepper, finely chopped
1 medium red onion, finely chopped
6 green onions, chopped
2 shallots, finely chopped
½ cup pitted imported black olives, thinly sliced
¼ cup chopped Italian parsley
½ cup chopped fresh dill
Salt and freshly ground black pepper to taste
1 package (10 ounces) peas (if desired, use 2 packages)

Whisk all the vinaigrette ingredients together in a bowl until blended.

Combine all the rice in a mixing bowl and pour in the vinaigrette. Toss and cool to room temperature. Add the remaining ingredients, except the peas, and toss.

Transfer to a large serving bowl. Arrange the peas in a circle on top, close to the edge of the bowl, for decoration.

Serve immediately or cover and refrigerate up to 3 hours. Serve at room temperature.

Danny Prince
Ladder 156, F.D.N.Y.

SPANISH-STYLE RICE WITH CHICKPEAS

This dish could also be done with little sausages (Libby's) instead of the chickpeas. It would then, of course, be called Spanish-Style Rice with Sausages.

SERVINGS: 4–6

1 onion, chopped
1 green pepper, chopped
1 tomato, chopped
¼ cup plus 3 tablespoons vegetable oil
1 can (8 ounces) tomato sauce
2 cans (15 ounces each) chickpeas
¼ jar small green stuffed olives (optional)
½ teaspoon dried oregano
1 tablespoon garlic powder
Black pepper
2 pounds long-grain white rice
Salt to taste

Sauté the onion, pepper, and tomato in the ¼ cup oil in a large pot. Add the tomato sauce and chickpeas (with a can of water). Add the olives (optional). Add the oregano, garlic powder, and black pepper and cook about 15 minutes over a low flame.

Rinse the rice, drain, and add to the pot. Add boiling water to come about ¾ inch over the rice. Make sure you stir rice while adding the water; otherwise it will come out soggy. Add salt and the 3 tablespoons oil and stir. Cook, uncovered, on a medium flame until the water disappears below the level of the rice. Stir the rice and cover. Cook on low about ½ hour, then stir again, replace the cover, and cook about ½ hour more.

Lillian Granieri
Bureau of Training, F.D.N.Y.

JOE LO CHEESY CONFETTI RICE

This makes a good side dish for a leg of lamb or for turkey.

SERVINGS: 6

¼ cup butter or margarine
1 cup long-grain white rice
¼ cup chopped onion
1 can (4 ounces) mild green chilies, drained
1 tablespoon instant chicken bouillon
2½ cups water
4 ounces Monterey Jack cheese, shredded
¼ cup pitted sliced ripe olives
1 jar (2 ounces) pimientos, drained and diced
1 tablespoon chopped fresh parsley

Melt the butter in a 2-quart saucepan. Add the rice and onion and cook over medium heat, stirring constantly, until the rice is a golden color, about 8 to 10 minutes. Add the green chilies and chicken bouillon, then add the water slowly. Bring the mixture to a full boil, 8 to 10 minutes. Reduce the heat to low, cover, and simmer for 25 to 30 minutes, or until the rice is tender. Stir in the remaining ingredients and serve immediately.

Joe Losinno
Engine 302, F.D.N.Y.

RICE BALLS

SERVINGS: MAKES 8 BALLS

2 cups cooked long-grain white rice
¼ cup grated Parmesan cheese
2 eggs
½ cup or more seasoned bread crumbs
Garlic powder to taste
1 tablespoon parsley flakes
1 tablespoon dried basil
Black pepper to taste
Vegetable oil

Combine all the ingredients except the oil in a bowl, mixing well with hands. Form into 8 balls.

Cover the bottom of a skillet with oil and heat over medium heat. Add the rice balls and fry on all sides until brown. Cool before serving.

NOTE: Add 4 ounces of ground meat, if desired. If so, add another ¼ cup grated cheese. With ground meat added, it makes 10 to 12 rice balls.

John Sineno, retired
Engine 58, F.D.N.Y.

POTATO PANCAKES

Serve these hot with applesauce and sour cream, or try ketchup and sweet relish.

SERVINGS: 8–10

5 pounds potatoes, peeled and shredded
4 to 5 large onions, chopped
4 cups all-purpose flour, or as needed
Salt and pepper to taste
½ teaspoon baking powder
2 eggs, beaten

Combine the potatoes, onions, flour, salt, pepper, and baking powder in a bowl. Blend in the beaten eggs. Add flour as needed, to create a mixture that's neither too stiff nor too loose.

Cover the bottom of a large black iron frying pan with oil. Heat over a medium flame. With a large spoon, drop the potato mixture into the hot oil. Allow to brown and then flip. Rotate to cook evenly. Drain on paper towels.

David Vredenburgh
Engine 248, F.D.N.Y.

POTATO BALLS

SERVINGS: 8

6 large potatoes, cooked, mashed, and cooled
2 eggs
¾ cup all-purpose flour
½ cup plain bread crumbs
¾ teaspoon salt

Place the cooled mashed potatoes in a covered bowl in refrigerator overnight.

The next day, add the eggs, flour, bread crumbs, and salt to the potatoes and mix well. Roll the mixture into balls about 1 to 1½ inches in diameter.

Bring a saucepan of water to a boil. Place the potato balls in boiling water. When they rise to the top (about 3 minutes), remove and serve.

Joe Bryant
Rescue 3, F.D.N.Y.

I thought it was kind of funny, actually, when my mother told me she was going to contribute a recipe to the first *Firefighter's Cookbook*. "But you don't cook anymore," I reminded her.

But she was excited about the idea, and welcomed the chance to honor her dear late mother by sending in Grandma's instructions for potato stuffing, a caloric orgy of mashed potatoes, fried onions, and ground beef.

Alice was delighted to see Grandma Betty's name and concoction in print, but alas, her own name was omitted. Despite her attempts to tell everyone in New York that the recipe on page 112 was hers, outside the F.D.N.Y. she remained the "unknown stuffer."

Now, as she celebrates fifteen years of service to the department, she is finally getting the fifteen minutes of fame she missed.

Linda Suslowitz-Federman
F.D.N.Y.

BETTY'S POTATO STUFFING

Use this to stuff a turkey or roasting chicken. Any mixture left over can be baked in a casserole in a 350° F oven for 30 minutes.

SERVINGS: 12

6 pounds potatoes
5 tablespoons butter or margarine
¼ cup milk
1 large onion, chopped
3 garlic cloves, chopped
1 pound ground meat, such as beef
Salt and pepper to taste
Garlic powder to taste
5 chestnuts, cooked and chopped (optional)

Peel, quarter, and boil the potatoes until tender, 20 to 30 minutes. Mash in a large bowl with 1 tablespoon of the butter and the milk. Brown onions and garlic in the remaining 4 tablespoons butter in a skillet. Add the ground meat and brown, breaking up the meat into small pieces. Add the meat mixture to mashed potatoes and season with salt, pepper, and garlic powder. Add the chestnuts, if using.

Alice Suslowitz
Bureau of Health Services, F.D.N.Y.

Bread AND Baked Goods

Sausage Bread/*Sineno*

Bishop's Bread/*Reed*

Cousin Jane's Polish Babka Bread/*Pinto*

Corcoran's Irish Soda Bread/*Corcoran*

Tolstoy's Carrot Muffins/*Kessler*

Firehouse Pancakes/*Santimauro*

French Toast Enfield/*Krempasky*

Grandma's Deep-fried French Toast/*Giuliani*

SAUSAGE BREAD

SERVINGS: 16–20

Dough:
1 package yeast
2 cups water
3 tablespoons vegetable oil
2 teaspoons salt
6 cups all-purpose flour

Filling:
6 to 7 medium onions, chopped
Vegetable oil
12 to 14 Italian sausages, meat removed from casings
1 small stick pepperoni, cut into small pieces
Salt to taste

Dissolve the yeast in ¼ cup of the water. When it's foamy, add to the rest of the water in a large bowl. Stir in the oil, salt, and flour. Turn out onto a board and knead until smooth. Let rise, covered, in a bowl until doubled, about 1 hour.

For the filling, sauté the onions in a little oil in a large skillet. When tender, add the sausage, pepperoni, and salt. Sauté till the sausage is thoroughly cooked.

Preheat the oven to 375° F.

Cut the dough into 5 or 6 pieces. Roll out each piece into a 12 x 8-inch rectangle. Spoon the filling over each dough rectangle and roll up; press the ends together to seal the roll. Place rolls, seam side down, on a greased baking pan. Bake for 1 hour, until the crust is golden brown. (You can baste each roll, while baking, with juice from the bottom of the pan.)

John Sineno, retired
Engine 58, F.D.N.Y.

BISHOP'S BREAD

SERVINGS: 10–12

2⅔ cups all-purpose flour, sifted
3 teaspoons baking powder
1 teaspoon salt
1 cup (packed) brown sugar
1 stick (½ cup) butter or margarine
2 eggs
1 cup milk

Crumb Topping:
½ cup sugar
½ cup all-purpose flour
½ stick (¼ cup) butter or margarine
1 teaspoon ground cinnamon

Preheat the oven to 375° F. Grease a 13 x 9 x 2-inch baking pan.

Sift together the flour, baking powder, and salt and set aside. In a large mixing bowl, beat the brown sugar and butter to blend well. Add the eggs and beat until the mixture is light and fluffy. Beat in the milk. Add the flour mixture and beat just till all the ingredients are combined. Turn the batter into the prepared pan.

For the topping, combine the sugar and flour with the butter and cinnamon to make crumbs. Sprinkle on top of the batter and bake for 25 minutes.

Mrs. Shirley Reed
Secretary to the Fire Commissioner, F.D.N.Y.

COUSIN JANE'S POLISH BABKA BREAD

SERVINGS: 16–20

Yeast Mixture:
2 packages yeast
½ teaspoon sugar
½ cup warm milk

Bread Mixture:
1½ cups milk
1½ sticks (¾ cup) butter
1 cup sugar
½ teaspoon salt
8 to 10 cups all-purpose flour, sifted
3 eggs
1½ cups golden raisins

Mix the yeast, sugar, and warm milk in a small bowl and let stand.

Scald the 1½ cups milk. While cooling, add the butter, sugar, and salt, stirring to melt the butter.

Stir the cooled milk into 5 cups of the flour in a large bowl; mix very well. Add the eggs and mix well, then add the yeast mixture and mix well.

Add the remaining flour as needed to make a nonsticking dough, mixing very well.

Flour bowl and dough—cover with a towel or blanket and keep in warm place away from draft. Let it rise, until doubled, then beat the dough down, cover, and let rise again. Beat the dough down, add the raisins, and mix well.

Preheat the oven to 350° F.

Place the dough in a greased pan (any shape desired, but large enough so the dough fills it just more than halfway). Let rise until almost doubled, then bake for 50 to 60 minutes.

Honorary Deputy Chief Joe Pinto
Engine 58/Ladder 26, F.D.N.Y.

CORCORAN'S IRISH SODA BREAD

SERVINGS: 7

1 stick (½ cup) margarine, melted
2½ cups all-purpose flour, sifted
½ cup sugar
1 teaspoon baking powder
½ teaspoon baking soda
Dash of salt
2 eggs
½ cup buttermilk
Raisins and caraway seeds (amount to your liking)

Preheat the oven to 325° F.

Mix the margarine, flour, sugar, baking powder, baking soda, and salt in a bowl using your hands. The mixture will be coarse.

Mix the eggs and buttermilk in a small bowl, then add to the flour mixture. Stir in the raisins and caraway seeds. Turn out onto a board and knead lightly until smooth.

Form the dough into a ball and place on a greased baking sheet. Cut a cross 1 inch deep in the top. Bake 1 hour and 15 minutes, or until browned. Check with a toothpick in the center; when it comes out dry, the bread is done.

Elaine Corcoran
In loving memory of "Big Jim" Corcoran
Ladder 19, Division 6, MSU/SOC, F.D.N.Y.

It's Easter time, and for this I submit the following. One might ask, "What do Tolstoy and Easter have in common?" To the best of my knowledge, absolutely nothing. However, the use of Tolstoy here, as the main subject, is quite simple. Again, I've cleverly, if I do say so myself, eluded personal attachment to yet another recipe. What's the title of "that" book again?

SERVINGS: ABOUT 12 MUFFINS

1 cup unbleached all-purpose flour
1 cup whole-wheat flour
1 teaspoon baking soda
1 teaspoon baking powder
¼ teaspoon ground nutmeg
1 teaspoon ground cinnamon
Pinch of salt
1 cup (lightly packed) brown sugar
¼ cup canola oil
2 eggs, at room temperature
2 teaspoons pure vanilla extract
⅓ cup Alaga brand cane syrup or dark corn syrup
1 tablespoon Amaretto (optional)
2 cups finely chopped carrots, lightly packed

Preheat the oven to 350° F.

Sift the first seven ingredients into a large mixing bowl; set aside. In a separate mixing bowl, whisk together the sugar, oil, and eggs. Incorporate the vanilla and cane syrup or corn syrup into this mixture. Blend in the Amaretto, if desired, and pour gradually into the dry ingredients, stirring constantly and gently with a wooden spoon. Fold in the carrots.

Lightly grease a 12-cup muffin pan and an ice-cream scoop (see note) with a cooking spray or canola oil. Fill the muffin pan, one scoop of dough per muffin, and bake for 15 to 18 minutes. Allow the muffins to cool. Twist, lift, and remove. Enjoy.

NOTE: The use of an ice-cream scoop is the best way to ensure that all the muffins will be the same size and therefore require identical cooking time. If you use a scoop with a release trigger, you're even better off, as the dough will come out quickly and cleanly when inverted over the muffin pan.

Warren G. Kessler, retired
Engine 268, F.D.N.Y.

FIREHOUSE PANCAKES

SERVINGS: 4–6

1⅓ cups milk
2 eggs, lightly beaten
1 stick (½ cup) butter, melted
2 cups sifted all-purpose flour
1 cup confectioners' sugar
4 tablespoons baking powder
½ teaspoon salt
Vegetable oil

Mix the milk, eggs, and butter in a small bowl. In another bowl, combine the flour, sugar, baking powder, and salt. Stir the milk mixture into the flour mixture until moistened.

Heat a lightly oiled griddle until hot. Spoon the mixture onto the griddle by ¼ cups and cook until bubbles appear evenly over the top of each pancake. Turn; cook on the second side until golden. Repeat until all the batter is used up.

Nick Santimauro
Ladder 166, F.D.N.Y.

F.D.N.Y. Buff

Mike "Enfield" Krempasky

A "buff" can be described as a person with a deep interest or love for a given subject. The subject could be anything from opera, history, or railroads to the fire department. A number of the F.D.N.Y. "buff" community are also members of a little-known organization called the Auxiliary Fire Corps. Termed "The Faithful," the Corps is intended to assist the Uniformed Force, F.D.N.Y., in times of natural or manmade disaster. Many of its members have the good fortune of being permitted to work in their company quarters, as well as responding on "runs" with the company.

For the members of F.D.N.Y. to allow a "buff," or auxiliary, to be a part of their world is a very special privilege. With most, to be accepted by the members as one of their own is not taken lightly. Being with a group of members for a length of time allows one to gain many insights into the life of a firefighter. One sees the reverence and respect for life, the sacrifice of life and limb for people they don't even know. The bonding and camaraderie among a group, a team that shares everything, good and bad. The well-honed sense of humor and straightforward way of being. The closeness and support that is intensified in times of tragedy. It's something you have to experience yourself to be truly able to grasp. It's wonderful, and it's something I wouldn't trade for anything in the world. Thanks, guys.

FRENCH TOAST ENFIELD

SERVINGS: 2–6

Skim milk, about 2½ cups
Lemon and orange extracts, about ¼ teaspoon each (or to taste)
2 eggs
Small amount of granulated sugar, if desired
Butter or margarine
8 to 10 slices challah or crusty round French bread, sliced about ¾ inch thick
Ground cinnamon
Confectioners' sugar
Nonfat ricotta cheese
Apricot halves
Honey or fruit preserves (optional)

Combine the milk, extracts, eggs, and granulated sugar in a wide, flat bowl. Whisk lightly until well mixed and slightly frothy.

Preheat a griddle until a drop of water dropped on the surface dances across and disappears. Then grease with about 1 tablespoon butter or margarine. Quickly dip both sides of the bread slices in the batter and place on the griddle. Turn the slices when lightly browned. While the other side browns, sprinkle the tops with cinnamon, then confectioners' sugar.

When the bottoms are lightly browned, remove the toast from the griddle and arrange on serving plates. Place a dollop of ricotta cheese at the side of each plate and garnish with apricot halves. If desired, top the slices with honey or fruit preserve of your choice.

Aux. Lt. Mike "Enfield" Krempasky
Auxiliary Fire Corps, F.D.N.Y.

GRANDMA'S DEEP-FRIED FRENCH TOAST

(A Favorite of Mayor Rudolph Giuliani's)

SERVINGS: 5

Vegetable oil
3 eggs, separated
3 tablespoons milk
2 teaspoons sugar
5 slices bread

Heat 2 inches of oil in a deep frying pan over a low flame.

Blend the egg yolks, milk, and sugar in a large bowl. In a second bowl, whip the egg whites to peaks, then fold gently into the yolk mixture.

Dip the bread, one slice at a time, into the batter to coat thickly. As the slices are coated, drop into the hot oil. Cook about 2 minutes on each side until golden brown.

Drain the French toast on paper towels and serve immediately with hot syrup, jam, or powdered sugar. No butter needed!

Donna Hanover Giuliani

Desserts

Cheesecake/*Bernard*

Italian Cheesecake/*Sineno*

Amaretto Cheesecake/*Sineno*

Piña Colada Cheesecake/*Sineno*

Pumpkin Cake/*Drennan*

Apple Cake/*Curry*

Apple Tart/*Bryant*

Top-Me-Twice Cake/*Walsh*

Lazy Daisy Cake/*Gerken*

The Dump Cake/*Finley*

Commissioner Howard Safir's Favorite Chocolate Cake/*Safir*

Chocolate "2" the Rescue/*Downey*

Sour Cream Coffee Cake/*Zuba*

Pumpkin Pie/*Zuba*

Pecan Pie/*Hafer*

Sweet Potato Pie/*Pinto*

Apple City Delight/*Manwaring*

Ole-Fashioned Creamy Rice Pudding/*Vredenburgh*

John Sineno's Famous No-Bake Rice Pudding/*Sineno*

Noodle Pudding/*McCue*

Italian Holiday Fig Cookies/*Sineno*

Rugelach/*Kessler*

Rum Balls/*Pinto*

Pistachio Mousse/*Sineno*

Honey Butter Brittle/*Kessler*

Dip for Fruit/*Freilinger*

Serve this plain or with some blueberry, strawberry, or cherry preserves, or with chopped walnuts. For chocolate fiends: Add 1½ cups mini chocolate chips to the filling before cooking.

SERVINGS: 12–16

Filling:
6 packages (8 ounces each) cream cheese
7 eggs
1½ cups sugar
1 tablespoon vanilla extract
1 tablespoon lemon juice
1 tablespoon all-purpose flour
1 cup half-and-half

Crust:
6 graham crackers, crushed
3 tablespoons butter, melted

Preheat the oven to 350° F.

For the crust, mix the crushed graham crackers and butter and pack firmly over the bottom of a 10-inch springform pan.

For the filling, all ingredients should be at room temperature. Beat the cream cheese with the eggs, one at a time, till smooth. Beat in the sugar, vanilla, lemon juice, and flour. Gently fold in the half-and-half.

Pour the batter over the graham cracker crust and bake for 1 hour. Turn the oven off and leave the cake in the oven for another hour until it cools. Refrigerate for at least 6 hours. Remove the sides of the pan before serving.

Frank Bernard
Ladder 26, Battalion 25, F.D.N.Y.

ITALIAN CHEESECAKE

SERVINGS: 12–16

4 packages (8 ounces each) cream cheese
1 container (16 ounces) ricotta cheese
5 or 6 eggs
1½ cups sugar
2 tablespoons cornstarch
½ stick (¼ cup) butter, melted
1 teaspoon vanilla extract
1 tablespoon anise extract
1 teaspoon coconut extract
1 teaspoon brandy extract
1 teaspoon orange extract
1 teaspoon rum extract
1 teaspoon lemon extract
1 teaspoon lemon juice
2 to 3 ounces chopped candied citron

Preheat the oven to 400° F.

Beat all the ingredients except the citron in a large bowl. When the batter is well mixed, pour into a blender; add the citron and blend thoroughly. Work in batches if necessary. Pour the batter into a greased 10- or 11-inch spring-form pan. Place the springform in a roasting pan half full of water and bake for 1 hour.

Let stand at room temperature for 2 hours, then refrigerate for 3 to 6 hours. Remove the sides of the pan before serving.

John Sineno, retired
Engine 58, F.D.N.Y.

AMARETTO CHEESECAKE

SERVINGS: 12–16

Filling:
4 packages (8 ounces each) cream cheese
1 container (16 ounces) sour cream
5 or 6 eggs
1½ cups sugar
2 tablespoons cornstarch
½ stick (¼ cup) butter, melted
1 tablespoon vanilla extract
1 tablespoon lemon juice
1 tablespoon almond extract
1 tablespoon orange extract
¼ cup Amaretto liqueur

Crust:
2½ cups crushed coconut crackers
1¼ sticks (⅔ cup) butter, melted

Up to 1 cup additional Amaretto

Preheat the oven to 400° F.

For the filling, beat all the ingredients in a large bowl to blend well and set aside.

Combine the crust ingredients and blend thoroughly. Reserving about a tablespoon of the crumbs, press the rest over the bottom of a greased 9-inch springform pan. Pour the batter over the crust, sprinkling the top with the reserved crumbs. Place the springform in a roasting pan half full of water and bake for 1 hour. After the cake is done, let it stand at room temperature for 2 hours. Remove the springform and invert the cake so that the bottom becomes the top. Transfer the cake into a pan with sides. Remove the bottom piece of the springform from what is now the top of the cake and pour Amaretto over the top, letting it soak in as desired. Transfer the cheesecake to a platter.

John Sineno, retired
Engine 58, F.D.N.Y.

PIÑA COLADA CHEESECAKE

I was sitting in the firehouse kitchen thinking of what meal to cook for the next tour. I asked the men what they would like. John Glynn popped up: "You've been experimenting with different cheesecakes on other tours, how about making one for us?" So I made a pineapple cheesecake for the brothers that day. John said, "This is it! What do you want to call it?" I said, "We'll call it XC-4." Experimental Cheesecake Number 4. Every time we had a "winner" we gave it a new number. We are now up to XC-24. This is a Piña Colada Cheesecake.

SERVINGS: 12–16

4 packages (8 ounces each) cream cheese
1 container (16 ounces) sour cream
5 or 6 eggs
1½ cups sugar
2 tablespoons cornstarch
½ stick (¼ cup) butter, melted
1 tablespoon vanilla extract
1 tablespoon lemon juice
1 teaspoon rum extract
1 cup flaked coconut
1 can (20 ounces) pineapple (tidbits or crushed), well drained

Preheat the oven to 400° F.

Beat all the ingredients except the coconut and pineapple in a large bowl. When the batter is well mixed, pour into a blender, add the coconut, and blend thoroughly. Work in batches if necessary. Pour the batter into a greased 9-inch springform pan and layer the drained pineapple on top. Place the springform in a roasting pan half full of water and bake for 1 hour. After the cake is done, let it stand at room temperature for 3 to 4 hours. Remove the sides of the pan before serving.

John Sineno, retired
Engine 58, F.D.N.Y.

In Memory of Capt. John Drennan, F.D.N.Y.

Vina Drennan

John Drennan's appetite was as big as his heart. To him a dish of ice cream meant a soup bowl. One of our daughters gave him one of those *Eating for a Healthy Heart* cookbooks and he was truly puzzled. He consistently confused hearty eating for healthy eating.

John loved being a firefighter, and of course one of the joys of the job was sharing the firehouse meals with people he respected and loved. I think firefighters are the only group of people that lose weight while on vacation. He loved soups and stews most of all, but he was easy to please. We never had any leftovers, and as long as his plate was full, he was happy.

After his funeral it was so hard to sit at the kitchen table, his empty chair sits so silently. We remember happier times and are so aware of how much we lost when John died. I've been invited to have some excellent dinners in firehouses this past year, and in my opinion there are no finer meals served anywhere.

In closing, I will always be grateful for the loving care received at the New York Hospital–Cornell Medical Center Burn Unit. My gratitude and appreciation goes out to the New York City Fire-fighters Burn Center Foundation for all the work they do to help others.

This is one of John's favorite recipes—pumpkin cake.

PUMPKIN CAKE

SERVINGS: 8–10

2 cups sugar
1¼ cups vegetable oil
1½ cups fresh pumpkin puree or canned pumpkin
4 eggs
3 cups all-purpose flour
2 teaspoons baking powder
2 teaspoons baking soda
2 teaspoons ground cinnamon
1 teaspoon salt
½ cup dark raisins
½ cup golden raisins
1 cup walnuts, chopped

Preheat the oven to 350° F.

Beat the sugar, oil, and pumpkin in a large bowl. Add the eggs, one at a time, beating well. Sift together the flour, baking powder, baking soda, cinnamon, and salt and stir into the pumpkin mixture. Fold the raisins and nuts into the cake batter.

Bake for 50 minutes in a lightly greased 9- or 10-inch tube pan.

Vina Drennan
F.D.N.Y.

APPLE CAKE

SERVINGS: 8–10

3 cups all-purpose flour
2 cups sugar
1 teaspoon baking soda
1 teaspoon ground cinnamon
1 teaspoon salt
3 cups diced apples
2 eggs, beaten
1 cup vegetable oil
1 teaspoon vanilla extract
2 cups chopped nuts

Preheat the oven to 350° F.

Combine the flour, sugar, soda, cinnamon, and salt in a large bowl, stirring to mix thoroughly. Make a well in the dry ingredients and add the apples, eggs, oil, and vanilla. Stir until mixed well. Stir in the chopped nuts.

Pour the batter into a 13 x 9 x 2-inch baking pan and bake for 45 minutes. Serve warm.

Capt. Joe Curry
Ladder 26, F.D.N.Y.

APPLE TART

SERVINGS: 4

6 McIntosh apples
1 unbaked 10-inch pastry shell
2 eggs
¼ cup sugar
½ cup heavy cream
½ cup milk

Preheat the oven to 350° F.

Core each apple and cut into 8 wedges. Arrange in the pie crust and bake for 20 minutes. Meanwhile, beat the remaining ingredients to mix well and pour over the apples. Bake 20 minutes longer.

Joe Bryant
Rescue 3, F.D.N.Y.

SERVINGS: 10

Cake:
2 cups all-purpose flour
1 cup sugar
1 teaspoon baking soda
1 teaspoon salt
1 can (13 ounces) crushed pineapple
1 teaspoon vanilla
2 eggs

Topping:
½ cup (packed) brown sugar
½ cup flaked coconut
½ cup chopped pecans

Sauce:
1 stick (½ cup) margarine
½ cup light cream
½ cup sugar
½ teaspoon vanilla extract

Preheat the oven to 350° F.

Combine all the cake ingredients in a bowl and beat for 2 minutes at low speed. Pour into a greased 9-inch square pan and bake for 45 minutes.

Meanwhile, in separate bowls, stir the topping ingredients to mix well and beat the sauce ingredients until smooth.

When the cake is done, remove it from the oven and pour first the topping and then the sauce over the cake. Return to the oven and bake for an additional 10 minutes. Cool and serve.

Eugene Walsh, Jr.
Engine 54, F.D.N.Y.

SERVINGS: 8

Cake:
2 eggs
1 cup sugar
1 teaspoon vanilla extract
1 cup all-purpose flour
2 teaspoons baking soda
½ cup milk, scalded and cooled
1 tablespoon butter

Topping:
¾ stick (6 tablespoons) butter
¼ cup evaporated milk or heavy cream
9 heaping tablespoons brown sugar
1 can flaked coconut

Preheat the oven to 350° F.

Beat the eggs in a bowl and add the sugar and vanilla. Beat until light and fluffy. Add the remaining ingredients one by one and continue to mix. Pour the batter into a greased 12 x 9 x 2-inch pan and bake for 20 minutes.

Meanwhile, melt the butter for the topping. Add the milk and sugar and blend. Fold in the coconut.

Remove the cake from the oven and spread with the topping. Return the cake to the oven and cook for an additional 3 to 5 minutes.

Former Chief Fred Gerken
Bellerose Village Fire Department, Bellerose, New York

THE DUMP CAKE

SERVINGS: 8–10

2 cans apple pie filling
1 can chunk pineapple, undrained
¾ cup raisins
2 sticks (1 cup) butter or margarine, melted
1 box yellow cake mix
1 cup crushed walnuts

Preheat the oven to 350° F.

Spread the apples and pineapple on the bottom of an ungreased 13 x 9 x 2-inch baking pan. Drop the raisins into the fruit mix. Sprinkle (do not mix) the dry cake mix evenly over the fruits. Pour the melted butter or margarine all over the cake mix and sprinkle with the walnuts. Bake for approximately 50 to 60 minutes.

Rosemary Finley
Friend of the Firefighter

COMMISSIONER HOWARD SAFIR'S FAVORITE CHOCOLATE CAKE

(a.k.a. Carol's Killer Cake)

Several years ago I found myself in a store waiting for the briefcase I had purchased for my husband's birthday to be monogrammed. I explained to the clerk that I was very short on time because I had to bake a chocolate cake for dessert. The clerk jotted down a recipe that has since become a family favorite. She guaranteed that it was the quickest, easiest, and most important, "chocolatiest" cake, although it has no frosting. I happily agree, and the cake she called "Inside-out Cake" has been keeping the commissioner sweet ever since!

SERVINGS: 8–10

1 package any brand devil's food cake mix
1 package instant chocolate pudding
1¾ cups milk
2 eggs
1 package (12 ounces) chocolate chips
Confectioners' sugar

Preheat the oven to 350° F. Well grease and flour a Bundt pan.

Combine the cake mix, chocolate pudding mix, milk, and eggs in a large bowl and beat with a wooden spoon about 50 strokes. Fold in the chocolate chips. Bake for about 45 to 55 minutes or until a toothpick in the center comes out clean. (Note: If the toothpick hits melted chocolate it will be moist.) When cool, dust with confectioners' sugar before serving.

NOTE: This cake travels well and keeps for a long time. Perfect to send to college students, at the holidays, etc.

VARIATIONS: Yellow or white cake, butterscotch bits for the chocolate chips. Have fun and enjoy!

Carol Safir
New York, New York

CHOCOLATE "2" THE RESCUE

SERVINGS: 20

1 package Oreo cookies
1 package regular fudge brownie mix
Chocolate syrup to cover
3 packages instant chocolate pudding
1 large container Cool Whip
Chocolate sprinkles

Place the Oreo cookies in a plastic bag and crush with a rolling pin. Set aside.

Make the brownies according to package directions and cool. Make holes all over the top of the brownies with a fork and pour on chocolate syrup to cover. Set aside to allow the syrup to be absorbed.

Make the chocolate pudding according to package directions.

In a large glass bowl make layers as follows: one third of the brownies (crumbled), one third of the chocolate pudding, one third of the Oreo cookies, and one third of the Cool Whip. Repeat the layers twice more and top with chocolate sprinkles.

Cover with plastic wrap and refrigerate for 2 to 3 days before serving. Enjoy!

Battalion Chief Ray Downey

SOUR CREAM COFFEE CAKE

SERVINGS: 12–14

1 cup butter or margarine, softened
2 cups sugar
1 container (16 ounces) sour cream
2 teaspoons baking soda
4 eggs
2 teaspoons vanilla extract
3 cups sifted all-purpose flour
3 teaspoons baking powder

Topping:
½ cup sugar
2 teaspoons ground cinnamon
½ cup chopped nuts
2 teaspoons unsweetened cocoa powder (more, if desired)

Preheat the oven to 350° F.

Beat the butter and sugar in a large bowl to blend well. Beat in the sour cream and baking soda. Add eggs, one at a time, beating well. Add the vanilla, flour, and baking powder and mix well. Pour the batter into a greased and floured 14½ x 10 x 2-inch baking pan or into two 8-inch square pans.

Mix the topping ingredients and sprinkle half this mixture over the batter; run a knife through to marbleize. Sprinkle the remaining topping over the blended batter and bake for 45 minutes.

Chuck Zuba
Ladder 26, F.D.N.Y.

Firefighting Family
(Cont.)

I was given an assignment to drive the Commissioner around to various functions and events. The car the Commissioner used was based where Engine 248 was housed. To warm up to the men in the firehouse, I made a couple of crumb cakes. At the end of the day, in returning to the firehouse, I met up with a chief who was having my crumb cake with a cup of coffee. For the life of him he couldn't remember which firehouse in Brooklyn he had last had this crumb cake. He said it was delicious, one of the best he'd ever tasted. He happened to look up and see me, and asked if I remembered him. "Sorry, Chief," I said, "you've changed over the years, and besides, you had that crumb cake in *Harlem* when we worked together many years ago!" We both laughed, but it was an honor for me to be remembered for something I had made so many years ago.

John Sineno

PUMPKIN PIE

SERVINGS: 8

1 cup (packed) brown sugar
1 tablespoon all-purpose flour
1 tablespoon pumpkin pie spice (or 1¼ teaspoons ground cinnamon, ½ teaspoon ground nutmeg, and ½ teaspoon ground ginger)
½ teaspoon salt
1 can (16 ounces) pumpkin or 2 cups fresh-cooked pumpkin puree
1 egg, slightly beaten
1 can (12 ounces) evaporated milk
1 unbaked deep-dish 9-inch pastry shell

Preheat the oven to 375° F.

Mix the brown sugar, flour, pumpkin pie spice, and salt in a large bowl. Add the pumpkin and blend till smooth. Stir in the egg and milk. Pour the mixture into the unbaked pastry shell and bake for 55 to 60 minutes, or until a knife inserted 2 inches from the edge comes out clean.

Chuck Zuba
Ladder 26, F.D.N.Y.

PECAN PIE

SERVINGS: 8

1 cup sugar
½ stick (¼ cup) butter, melted
4 eggs
2 tablespoons dark rum
1 tablespoon vanilla extract
¾ cup light corn syrup
½ cup dark corn syrup
8 ounces pecans, halved
1 frozen 9-inch pie shell

Preheat the oven to 350° F.

Blend the sugar and butter together in a bowl. Stir in the eggs, rum, vanilla, and corn syrups. Pour the pecans into the pie shell and pour the syrup mixture over. Bake for about 50 minutes, or until golden brown.

Carol B. Hafer
Counsel to F.D.N.Y.

SWEET POTATO PIE

SERVINGS: 2 PIES (8 SERVINGS EACH)

4 or 5 medium yams, scrubbed (not peeled)
2 eggs
2 teaspoons vanilla extract
1 cup (packed) brown sugar
½ cup white sugar
½ can milk
Ground cinnamon, nutmeg, and allspice to taste
2 unbaked 9-inch pie shells

Preheat the oven to 350° F.

Boil the yams in a large pot until tender. Drain and cool under cold running water. Peel the yams, put in a bowl, and mash with a mixer, removing any strings. Add all the remaining ingredients, except of course the pie shells, one at a time, blending well.

Pour the batter into the pie shells and bake for about 45 minutes to 1 hour.

Honorary Deputy Chief Joe Pinto
Engine 58/Ladder 26, F.D.N.Y.

APPLE CITY DELIGHT
(Microwavable Apple Crisp)

SERVINGS: 6

8 medium apples, peeled, cored, and sliced
2 tablespoons lemon juice
5 tablespoons (⅓ cup) butter or margarine, softened
¾ cup (packed) brown sugar
½ cup all-purpose flour
½ cup quick-cooking rolled oats
½ teaspoon ground cinnamon

Toss the apples with the lemon juice in an 8-inch microwavable baking dish. In a bowl, combine the remaining ingredients with a fork until crumbly. Sprinkle over the apples. Microwave, uncovered, on high power 10 to 12 minutes, or until the apples are tender.

Ron Manwaring
Apple City Fire Department, Murphysboro, Illinois

Engine 91 often responds to the same alarms as Engine 58. One morning, as both companies were repacking their hoses after a small tenement fire, one of the men from Engine 91 asked if I'd make them a tray of rice pudding that they might have with their lunch. I said I'd be glad to and would start on it as soon as I got back to quarters.

Knowing my guys, I knew they'd also want rice pudding if I made a tray for Engine 91, so I decided to make two trays of pudding instead of one.

When the puddings were done, I left both trays on the kitchen table to cool and went upstairs to wash up. Ed Fealey couldn't resist the temptation to pull a gag. While I was upstairs, Fealey put some spoons, forks, and knives into one of the trays of pudding, where they naturally sank to the bottom.

When I returned to the kitchen, I topped off the pudding with cinnamon and called Engine 91 to tell them that they could pick up their pudding whenever they were ready.

Shortly thereafter we received another alarm, to which Engine 91 also responded. They were dismissed from the scene before we were, so they decided to stop by our firehouse on the way back to theirs and pick up their tray of pudding.

A few days later we caught another job along with Engine 91. After the fire had been extinguished and we were "taking up," I asked one of the guys from Engine 91 if they had enjoyed the pudding.

"John, it was great. But how did you know that we needed silverware?" he replied.

I didn't know what he was talking about and thought about it all the way back to quarters. It wasn't until we got back and were having a cup of coffee in the kitchen that Ed Fealey could no longer restrain his mirth and blurted out his silverware caper. He professed complete innocence, however, in extending the gag to include the guys at 91.

"I played the joke on our guys. How was I to know it would ricochet?" he said.

John Sineno

OLE-FASHIONED CREAMY RICE PUDDING

SERVINGS: 8–10

1 quart whole milk
¼ teaspoon salt
1 cup long-grain white rice, rinsed in cold water and drained
2 eggs
1 cup evaporated milk
1 teaspoon vanilla
½ cup sugar
½ cup raisins, soaked in boiling water for 15 minutes and drained
Ground nutmeg

Combine the milk and salt in a large saucepan and heat. When the milk is warm, add the rice. Bring to a slow boil and then reduce to a simmer, stirring occasionally. Cook till the rice is soft, about 45 minutes, stirring occasionally.

Meanwhile, in a large bowl blend the eggs, ¾ cup of the evaporated milk, the vanilla, and sugar. Set aside.

Add the remaining ¼ cup evaporated milk to the rice. Stir, then add the raisins. The mixture should be thickening. When the rice is soft, spoon 1 cup of the rice mixture into the egg mixture, stir, and then slowly pour the egg mixture into the remaining rice. Cook until it becomes bubbly and thick, stirring frequently. Pour into a bowl and sprinkle with nutmeg. Serve warm or cold.

David Vredenburgh
Engine 248, F.D.N.Y.

A Rice Pudding Story

I was asked to do a charitable event for drug rehabilitation and prepare some of my desserts. I set up the desserts, which were at the end of a horseshoe table with the rest of the foods. I had prepared rice pudding, icebox cake, and cheesecake. This little old woman is making her way down the line and asking what's this, what's that, etcetera. I told her this was icebox cake, this was cheesecake, and this was rice pudding, would she like some? She shook her head vigorously

I said, "Don't you like rice pudding?"

She replied that she loved it, but that she would only eat *one* rice pudding. "I watched a fireman on television making the rice pudding. I have that recipe, and it's the only one I like," she said.

I answered, "I wouldn't say that if I were you—you'll eat this rice pudding, you'll *like* this rice pudding, because I am that fireman!"

John Sineno

JOHN SINENO'S FAMOUS NO-BAKE RICE PUDDING

SERVINGS: 20–25

1 pound long-grain white rice
1 gallon milk
3 cups sugar
3 ounces vanilla extract
2 cans (12 ounces each) evaporated milk
1 package vanilla tapioca pudding (not instant)
5 eggs, beaten
Raisins (optional—as many or as few as you want)
Ground cinnamon

In a large saucepan with a lid, cook the rice, milk, and sugar, stirring occasionally, until the mixture comes to a slow boil. Reduce the flame and let it simmer—and remember, stirring prevents a mixture from sticking. As the mixture begins to thicken, add the vanilla, evaporated milk, and tapioca pudding. Stir well and cover.

Very slowly and gradually, add the eggs to the simmering mixture. Cook, stirring, until thickened.

If raisins are to be added, place in a bowl, cover with boiling water, and let stand 15 minutes; drain. Put the raisins in the bottom of a large baking pan (or two disposable foil baking pans), pour the pudding over the raisins, stir, then let the mixture cool.

Sprinkle the top of the rice pudding with cinnamon before serving.

John Sineno, retired
Engine 58, F.D.N.Y.

NOODLE PUDDING

SERVINGS: 4–6

Pudding:
8 ounces wide noodles, cooked and drained
¾ stick (6 tablespoons) margarine
1 package (3 ounces) cream cheese, softened
¾ cup milk
¼ cup sugar
3 eggs, well beaten
1 small can apricot nectar
½ cup raisins

Topping:
1 cup corn flake crumbs
1 teaspoon cinnamon
¼ cup sugar
½ stick (¼ cup) margarine

Preheat the oven to 350° F.

Mix the noodles with the margarine, cream cheese, milk, sugar, eggs, apricot nectar, and raisins. Pour into a greased 11 x 7 x 2-inch baking dish.

Combine the topping ingredients with a fork until crumbly and sprinkle over the pudding. Bake 50 to 60 minutes.

Joe McCue, retired
F.D.N.Y.

ITALIAN HOLIDAY FIG COOKIES

The older the better, these cookies will last about a month.

SERVINGS: 10 COOKIES

2 packages (8 ounces each) figs on string, chopped
2 packages (8 ounces each) dates, chopped
1 can (8 ounces) slivered almonds
1 pound honey
1 cup water
Black pepper
4 packages pie crust mix

Preheat the oven to 375° F.

Chop the figs and dates and add the almonds. Combine the honey and water and cook about 30 minutes until soft. Add the dates, figs, almonds, and black pepper to the honey. Let cool. Prepare the dough and roll into 5 x 10-inch rectangles. Spoon the fruit and honey mixture onto half of each rectangle. Fold the dough over the mixture. Cut diagonally. Bake for 10 minutes. Cool.

John Sineno, retired
Engine 58, F.D.N.Y.

RUGELACH

Pastry:
1 pound sweet butter, softened
2 packages (8 ounces each) cream cheese, softened
4 cups all-purpose flour
Confectioners' sugar

Filling:
Chocolate chips
Raisins
Strawberry jam
Crushed walnuts

Mix the butter and cream cheese into the flour until blended. Divide the dough into four parts. Wrap each portion of dough in wax paper and refrigerate for approximately 2 hours.

Preheat the oven to 375° F.

Remove the dough from refrigerator, one portion at a time. Dust your work surface with confectioners' sugar and roll out the dough about ⅛ inch thick. While rolling out the dough, add confectioners' sugar as you would flour when needed.

Cut the rolled dough into 3-inch triangles. Add any combination of fillings or all by creating a mixture, approximately 1 teaspoon to the center of each triangle. Overlap the edges of the triangles to close, pinching to seal.

Place the rugelach on a cookie sheet and bake for 20 minutes. Cool on racks.

Repeat with the remaining portions of dough.

Milton Kessler, retired
Transfer Assignments Office Headquarters, F.D.N.Y.

RUM BALLS

SERVINGS: 2 DOZEN RUM BALLS

2½ cups vanilla wafer crumbs (about 8 ounces)
1 cup pecans, chopped
2 tablespoons unsweetened cocoa powder
¼ cup light corn syrup
¼ cup rum
Confectioners' sugar

Mix the vanilla wafers and chopped nuts in a bowl. Add the cocoa powder, corn syrup, and rum; mix well. Coat your hands with confectioners' sugar and roll the mixture into balls ½ to ¾ inch in diameter. Refrigerate for about 1 hour; roll in confectioners' sugar and serve.

Joe Pinto
Engine 58, F.D.N.Y.

PISTACHIO MOUSSE

SERVINGS: 4–6

2 packages pistachio pudding and pie filling (see note)
2¼ cups whipped cream or Cool Whip
1 cup milk
Handful of chocolate chips

Mix all the ingredients together and refrigerate.

NOTE: You can use any of the following instant pudding flavors: chocolate chip, chocolate mint, butter almond, vanilla, toasted coconut, or banana cream.

John Sineno, retired
Engine 58, F.D.N.Y.

One day Danny Prince, Ladder 156, called me and said, "John, I need a few recipes to include in a cookbook. It's a fund-raiser for Father Brady." I said I'd be glad to help; I'd even bake a few cakes for the event. Gerard O'Donnell, executive assistant to the Fire Commissioner, came up to me a few days later and asked to have his name on one of the cakes I was baking for the church fund-raiser. I told him that would be no problem, and on a pistachio chocolate chip mousse I put the initials G.O.D.

Several weeks after the event I met Danny and asked if everything went all right. Danny assured me that the fund-raiser was a big success, but then drew me aside and asked: "Was the mousse marked **GOD** intended as some special gesture for Father Brady?"

When I stopped laughing, I told him it was the abbreviation for *G*erard *O'D*onnell.

John Sineno

HONEY BUTTER BRITTLE

SERVINGS: 10

1 cup walnuts, coarsely chopped
2 sticks (1 cup) butter
½ cup (packed) brown sugar
½ cup honey
Dash of salt
1 teaspoon vanilla extract

Toast the walnuts by spreading on a baking sheet and heating in a 350° F oven for 10 minutes, stirring frequently. Set aside.

In a large saucepan combine the butter, brown sugar, honey, and salt. Bring to a boil, stirring. Add ½ cup of the nuts and continue cooking on *low*, stirring frequently to the hard-crack stage (see note). Add the vanilla.

Pour the candy into a well-buttered 8-inch-square baking pan. Cover the top with the remaining walnuts and press in.

When the candy is cold, turn out of the pan and break into small, irregular pieces.

NOTE: 300° F on a candy thermometer; rushing this procedure will only cause the mixture to burn. If no thermometer is available, put cold water in a glass and drop a small amount of the mixture into water. If the candy forms a hard, brittle thread, it is done.

Warren G. Kessler, retired
Engine 268, F.D.N.Y.

DIP FOR FRUIT

SERVINGS: 8

Assorted fruits
1 package (3 ounces) cream cheese
1 jar (7 ounces) marshmallow creme
1 ounce Kahlúa (see note)

Prepare selected fruits (e.g., strawberries, sliced kiwi, pineapple chunks, banana slices, orange sections, etc.). Set aside.

Combine the cream cheese and marshmallow creme and mix thoroughly. Add the Kahlúa and chill. Serve in a small bowl, surrounded by the fruit.

NOTE: Other liqueurs may be substituted, e.g., Frangelico, Vandermint, Amaretto, etc.

J. Joseph Freilinger
West Des Moines Volunteer, Des Moines, Iowa

RECIPE FOR A FIREFIGHTER
IN MEMORY OF CAPT.
JAMES F. MCDONNELL

Ingredients:

Active play	Humility
Humor	Courage
Wisdom	Patience
Endurance	Glaze of love
Strength	

Set aside a small child.

Sprinkle generously with active play to mold a strong body.

Add liberally, stirring slowly, huge handfuls of humor—a firefighter will not jell without it.

Watch carefully for approximately 13 years until the child turns into a spirited youth.

Add the seeds of wisdom that only grow through youthful trial and error.

Knead continuously through the teen years until endurance is blended with strength.

Add slowly the yeast of humility.

Set aside for 3 or 4 years, allowing the dough time to rise and double.

Call in master chefs with the recipe engraved upon their hearts for the final work.

Punch down the fully risen dough to shape the loaf.

Roll carefully, using the rolling pin of training on the well-floured board of discipline.

Blend in the rare spice of courage found hidden between the leaves of foolishness and cowardice that is only purchased with the gold of sacrifice.

Shape the loaf with care, and brush with the glaze of love to make them shine.

It is this glaze of love for human life that makes them what they are. The love that makes them stand and risk life, health, and security for strangers until their job is done, and they hear these precious words:

"Well done—good and faithful servant."

NOTE: Firefighters are prepared and blended only over many years.

Betty Lines
December 1985

Firefighter John Sineno
Engine 58, F.D.N.Y.

An award-winning cook and author of *The Firefighter's Cookbook,*
John Sineno is one of the most well-respected and best-known
firehouse chefs in America. John earned the nickname "Mama
Sineno" because he looks after his firefighting "family" as if he
were their mom. Though his days of putting out fires are over, he
hasn't hung up his apron and continues to endear a younger gen-
eration of firefighters with his extraordinary culinary talents.
"Walking into the firehouse for the first time was a rather strange
experience," John says. "I was concerned about starting off on the
right foot, but the only question the captain asked me was 'Can you
cook?'"

Index